ISBN 978-1-397-30883-2
PIBN 11375281

U.S. NATIONAL
LIBRARY
OF
MEDICINE

OUTLINES FOR PSYCHIATRIC EXAMINATIONS

Revised by

NOLAN D. C. LEWIS, M. D.

Director, New York State Psychiatric Institute and Hospital, New York

THIRD EDITION

Published by

THE NEW YORK STATE
DEPARTMENT OF MENTAL HYGIENE
ALBANY, N. Y.

1943
c. 2

PRINTED IN U. S. A.
STATE HOSPITALS PRESS
UTICA, N. Y.

CONTENTS

CONTENTS

PREFACE

The present volume is a revision of the Guides for History Taking and Clinical Examination of Psychiatric Cases edited in 1921 by Dr. George H. Kirby, then Director of the Psychiatric Institute. Widespread use of the first edition has reaffirmed the soundness of the principles of psychiatric history taking and clinical examination laid down by Dr. Adolf Meyer. The first edition was based largely on those principles and they have been retained in the present edition.

The first edition was compiled mainly for the use of physicians in psychiatric hospitals. Since 1921, however, with the spread and advance of psychiatric education and interest, the Guides have been more widely used by medical students and psychiatrists in various psychiatric activities. In the present edition, therefore, certain revisions and amplifications have been made with such uses in mind.

The outline for the study of the family and personal history has been rearranged and modified to include the study of the personality. This inclusion has been considered advisable because of the feeling that the individual is best understood when the facts of his personality are studied with the events of his life. Experience has shown that attempts to study personality detached from the events of the patient's life may give static pictures and fail to differentiate between the more normal or usual personality reactions and those which are a part of the psychiatric disorder. In the present personal history outline the aim is, therefore, to connect closely the events of the patient's life at different periods and his reaction to them. However, the outline for personality studies based largely on the work of Hoch and Amsden has been retained for those who prefer to follow it.

In the present edition a new section on the psychiatric examination of children has been added.

The classification of psychiatric disorders approved by the American Psychiatric Association, with definitions and explanatory notes compiled by the Editor, has been included in the present edition for the assistance of those using the Outlines. The classification of psychiatric disorders in children, with definitions and explanatory notes compiled by Brown, Pollock and Potter, has also been incorporated, with some modifications.

The Editor acknowledges the helpful suggestions given in the revision of the Guides by Dr. Richard H. Hutchings, Dr. Paul C. Taddiken and Dr. George W. Mills.

Dr. Howard W. Potter and Dr. Leland E. Hinsie, materially assisted the Editor in the revision of the Guides.

August, 1934 CLARENCE O. CHENEY.

PREFACE TO SECOND EDITION

It is gratifying to learn that this book has been helpful to physicians, medical students and others who are faced with the task of the examination of psychiatric patients, and that a second printing has become necessary. Minor changes have been made with attempts at further clarification but it has not been thought necessary to change the general arrangement or plan of the book. Because of certain suggestions that have been made for alterations, it seems advisable to call attention to the fact that this book is not to be looked upon as a textbook of psychiatry, nor does it aim to define all of the psychiatric terms that might be used. Other publications are of course available for such purposes.

In response to comments regarding the classification of psychiatric disorders included in this book, attention is also called to the fact that the Editor is not responsible for this classification which was arrived at after careful consideration by representatives of the American Psychiatric Association and the American Neurological Association and accepted by both associations as an official classification and was published accordingly in the Standard Nomenclature of Disease. The editor therefore has not presumed to make changes in this classification which obviously may not satisfy entirely the wishes of those who have to use it. He is responsible only for the explanatory notes which have been formulated to meet as far as seems possible the needs of the classification.

CLARENCE O. CHENEY.

White Plains, New York.
August, 1938.

ges, medical students and others who are need le of the examination of psychiatric patients, second printing has become necessary. Minor e been made with attempts at further clarifica- has not been thought necessary to change the rangement or plan of the book. Because of gestions that have been made for alterations, it isable to call attention to the fact that this book be looked upon as a textbook of psychiatry nor to define all of the psychiatric terms that might Other publications are of course available for ses.

nse to comments regarding the classification of disorders included in this book, attention is to the fact that the Editor is not responsible for fication which was arrived at after careful con- by representatives of the American Psychiatric and the American Neurological Association ted by both associations as an official classi- nd was published accordingly in the Standard ture of Diseases. The editor therefore has not to make changes in this classification which obvi- not satisfy entirely the wishes of those who have He is responsible only for the explanatory notes e been formulated to meet as far as seems possible of the classification.

Clarence O. Cheney.

lains, New York.
1938.

PREFACE TO THIRD EDITION

These "Outlines" do not include many of the special methods which have been devised for exhaustive studies in mental diseases, but they are intended as were former editions to direct the attention of the examiner along the important channels in mental history-taking, to refer to the special topics and factors to be investigated, and to serve as an orderly scheme for the examination of psychiatric patients. Many of the suggestions will not apply in each individual case, but they are offered to include the numerous possibilities which may be encountered in the various phases and types of mental disorder.

The general form of the book and the order of the contents have been retained. Some sections have not been changed, but other parts have been deleted and still others modified considerably. Some parts of the classification of psychiatric disorders are in need of revision, but as it is the official classification of the American Psychiatric Association and of the Standard Classified Nomenclature of Disease any changes at this time would interfere seriously with statistical work under way in several centers.

I wish to acknowledge the valuable aid given by Dr. Joseph Zubin of the psychology department of the Psychiatric Institute in writing the sections dealing with psychological tests and their evaluations, and by Miss Florence Brierley in the preparation of the manuscript.

Gratitude is also expressed to the following publishers who kindly permitted the use of certain excerpts from their publications: Journal of Psychology, Carl Murchison, publisher; The Williams and Wilkins Company; Psychological Corporation; Journal of Applied Psychology published by The American Psychological Association.

October, 1943. NOLAN D. C. LEWIS.

EFACE TO THIRD EDITION

"Outlines" do not include many of the special which have been devised for exhaustive studies in iseases, but they are intended as were former edi- direct the attention of the examiner along the in- hannels in mental history taking, to refer to the opics and features to be investigated, and to serve derly scheme for the examination of psychiatric Many of the suggestions will not apply in each l case, but they are offered to include the numer- ibilities which may be encountered in the various nd types of mental disorder.

neral form of the book and the order of the contents n retained. Some sections have not been changed, e parts have been deleted and still others modified ly. Some parts of the classification of psychi- orders are in need of revision, but as it is the official tion of the American Psychiatric Association and tandard Classified Nomenclature of Disease any at this time would interfere seriously with statisti- under way in several centers.

to acknowledge the valuable aid given by Dr. aubin of the psychology department of the Psychi- titute in writing the sections dealing with psycho- ests and their evaluations, and by Miss Florence in the preparation of the manuscript.

ude is also expressed to the following publishers lly permitted the use of certain excerpts from their ons: Journal of Psychology, Carl Murchison, pub- he Williams and Wilkins Company; Psychological tion: Journal of Applied Psychology published by

THE USE OF GUIDES IN CLINICAL PSYCHIATRY

The necessity of following some kind of a plan or method of case-study in psychiatric work is universally recognized. Physicians taking up psychiatry should, therefore, first of all, try to perfect themselves in the art of history taking and strive to develop an efficient technique for the examination of mental patients. Facility and skill will be acquired slowly and only after painstaking effort. Method and technique are just as important in psychiatry as in any branch of internal medicine or clinical diagnosis.

Owing to the variety and complexity of the situations dealt with in the investigation of life histories and the difficulties encountered in the examination of many types of mental disorder, the student or physician who approaches a case without a definite plan in mind is certain to overlook important facts or permit the patient to lead too much in the examination, often with the result that the time is not spent to the best advantage or that he is misled into drawing false conclusions.

One of the chief obstacles in developing a satisfactory scheme has lain in the difficulty of devising guides that would meet the requirements of the widely differing types of cases and not at the same time be too cumbersome and involved for practical clinical application. Furthermore, the kind of guidance needed by one beginning psychiatric work is quite different from that required by an experienced clinician. One unfamiliar with the guides presented in the following pages will perhaps at first feel that they are too elaborate and go too much into detail; especially is this likely to be the reaction of one who must examine fairly rapidly a large number of cases, a situation which, unfortunately, often confronts physicians in large admission services. The fact that work must sometimes be done under conditions unfavorable for the best and most satisfactory results furnishes no valid reason for objection to a method which aims at a higher level of thoroughness and completeness.

The guides present in some detail the various topics which it is essential to keep in mind if cases are to be carefully and adequately studied. It is not expected that one would, even under ideal conditions, undertake to follow out in every case each line of inquiry suggested in the various guides. They contain a good deal of information and various tests which should be available when needed. One's experience and judgment must decide how far it is desirable or necessary to push the examination in this or that direction. The student and physician new to psychiatry who have not had such experience as to acquire sharp clinical judgment do well to carry out the examinations in detail in the topics outlined and thus avoid the errors in diagnosis and suggestions for treatment which even experienced physicians will fall into if conclusions are drawn from a superficial, unsystematic examination. It is better for the physician and for the patient to get more facts than are absolutely essential than to miss important facts through overconfidence in one's diagnostic judgment. Thorough familiarity with the guides and the general plan of study outlined will give the student and physician a solid foundation on which to develop psychiatric technique and clinical skill and will qualify him to make special clinical studies and investigations as opportunities arise.

THE ANAMNESIS

(Synopsis)

a. Introduction

b. Informant

c. Family History

d. Personal History

1. Infancy
2. Childhood
3. Adolescence
4. Adult Life
5. Previous Attacks of Mental Disorder
6. Onset and Symptoms of the Psychiatric Disorder

II

THE ANAMNESIS

a. *Introduction.* In the study of psychiatric patients a good account of the previous history of the patient, the physical and mental development, and the manner in which the disorder began is very important. Without this information it will be quite impossible in many cases to understand the nature of the disorder or to make a satisfactory diagnostic grouping or to outline treatment.

Every mentally-ill person is a special problem in diagnosis and treatment. Every mental patient is a unity, a unique example, suffering from some particular combination of events that has broken or is breaking his adaptations to life. The first task of the physician in determining the cause or the nature of the illness is the collection of pertinent data.

Securing the record of the subjective complaints and the physical examination of the patient are arts, the systematic method of sorting and classifying the data and the making of a diagnosis from the facts secured is a science, and treatment is a combination of science and art. Errors in judgment, errors in analysis, errors in data, and above all errors in technique are among the reasons or sources of a mistaken diagnosis.

A desirable history is one which is complete and yet concise. Long descriptions are not necessarily clear accounts.

The practice should be to try always to get the anamnesis from relatives or friends, as in many instances one cannot depend on the patient for the previous history as is usually done in general medical cases. It is therefore essential to devote as much time and care as possible to the obtaining of full and reliable statements from visitors. It requires time and experience to become proficient in this aspect of psychiatric work. A number of interviews with the same informant, or with different members of the family, or friends, will in most cases be necessary in order to obtain a correct estimate of the family stock and traits and to get a satisfactory account of the patient's life and mental breakdown. It is particularly difficult to obtain a good anamnesis by means of correspondence or through attendants, although the latter often do very well if they have had training in the observation of patients. Experience has shown that trained psychiatric social workers may often be of great assistance in getting histories and the physician should not neglect to utilize to the fullest extent the services of the social worker in securing the desired information. History taking by the student or younger physicians is advocated, however, as an important part of their training. Visits to the homes of their patients by students for first hand knowledge of the family and social setting in which the patients have lived are likewise advocated as a helpful part of their training.

In the following pages various important lines of inquiry are taken up under certain general headings. This is done for the purposes of convenience and systematic approach, but the sequence suggested need not in all cases be followed.

Because of the frequent immediate concern of relatives with the patient's illness, it often facilitates the taking of an anamnesis to get first the account of the present illness, with all the details, then inquire about the personal history, leaving the family history until last. In recording the findings in the case history, however, the order indicated in the guide should be followed.

Before the anamnesis is considered complete, all of the topics mentioned should be covered by an appropriate inquiry.

The use of short summarizing headings for the different paragraphs or topics is advised, as these render it easy to get rapidly the salient facts from a case history. The headings should, however, be brief and concise and not simply a somewhat shorter statement of what is to follow in the paragraph.

In hospital cases where there are no relatives or visitors or in clinic cases where only the patient is seen and the patient must give the previous history, it is advised that this be recorded in the usual form of an anamnesis and be placed, as is customary, in the front part of the case record rather than incorporated in that division of the mental status dealing with memory tests and the patient's ability to give personal data. In some cases it will, of course, not be possible to take an anamnesis from the patient until the more disturbed phase of the psychosis has subsided or even until convalescence has set in. Case histories often lose a great deal of their value because no anamnesis was obtained from the patient before discharge or from the visitor who came to take the patient home.

It is suggested that the student or physician always study the anamnesis guide thoroughly and have the topics clearly in mind or notes of them to guide him when relatives or other visitors are interviewed in hospitals or the patients in clinics. This method is considered preferable to the distracting use of the guide itself during interviews. In dealing with hospitalized patients the physician should have at hand the following:

1. Copy or abstract of legal paper by which the patient was admitted. It is important to go over the statements of the relatives and the patient contained in the paper. Very often relatives deny statements made to the committing physicians or give quite a different account of happenings preceding the patient's admission than that recorded in the commitment paper.

2. The report of the examination of the patient, if this has been made, including his account of his life and illness so that the statements of the patient and informants may be compared and evaluated. Conflicting information may be gotten from the different sources and every effort should be made by careful inquiry to arrive at the truth. Not infrequently this goal may be reached only by inquiry from unrelated, disinterested persons, but in making such in-

quiries due regard should always be given to the confidential relationship of patient and physician.

3. The statistical data sheet. This should be filled in as far as possible at the time the anamnesis is taken because many of the items require special inquiry if accurate statistical data are to be obtained. It is also important to complete as much of the data sheet at this first interview as possible because of certain information called for in death certificates, in questions of legal residence, in deportation proceedings, etc.

THE ANAMNESIS

Name of patient Hospital or clinic number:

Taken by Date

b. INFORMANT:

1. Name
2. Address Telephone number
3. Relationship to patient
4. Intelligence and reliability

Record mental or physical characteristics observed in the informant and other relatives seen. Subsequent family history and observations made of relatives may be recorded as an addition to the family history and inserted in the case record.

c. FAMILY HISTORY:

The family history furnishes evidence of hereditary factors as well as the environmental influences. It is a record of the germ plasm. It may disclose inherited diseases or tendencies to certain disorders. There is no "negative" or "negligible" family history. Every animal and plant breeder recognizes the importance of differentiating strong and weak strains, likewise the physician should learn the character of the stock from which the patient is derived. Is it a long-lived stock or are the majority of the antecedents short-lived? Is it a healthy or sickly family?

The value of the existing statistics on heredity in nervous and mental disorders, "temperaments," and personality traits is greatly impaired (sometimes to the extent that they are worthless) by reason of the fact that the investigator has failed to differentiate true germ plasm inheritance from the identification traits which are of universal expression during the time of childhood relationships with the parents or other relatives; in other words, the child at a very early age introjects or makes a part of his own pattern of behavior the character traits, motor habits, and mental characteristics of his "contact" persons and other contemporaries. These identifications find their way into and are included in statistics on suicide and various other family developments.

Reliable information on matters of inheritance in the human family is exceedingly difficult to obtain, even when such information exists, as the feeling of disgrace to the family all too frequently obtains and is of widespread distribution, not only in connection with nervous and mental disorders but with diabetes, tuberculosis, and particularly with cancer and syphilis. The following suggestions, if followed out, render investigations in heredity a tedious procedure and often postpone the final evaluation, but when carried to a conclusion the result is a reliable history of hereditary factors.

a. Information on the family history in any given case should be taken, if possible, from:

1. the individual under investigation
2. a parent, sibling, or other near relative
3. a distant relative, preferably one who is not on good terms with the family
4. the family physician or clergyman
5. a neighbor or other person who has known the family for a number of years

This information should be as complete as possible in regard to nervous and mental conditions, temperament and character, diabetes, tumors, tuberculosis, syphilis, asthma and hay fever, hypertension, occupation, and nativity. In fact, it would be advisable to determine any obvious tendencies toward the development of any type of disease process any place in the family line.

b. A note accompanying the information should state the age, social level, and economic status of the informant, and the examiner's impression of his reliability.

c. The information from each informant may then be divided into:

1. that given voluntarily
2. that given on interrogation
3. that given reluctantly

d. The statements should then be grouped as to the degree of authenticity:

1. unquestionable facts
2. probabilities
3. possibilities

e. In recording some of the more interesting cases showing significant family histories, a heredity chart may be constructed utilizing the standard symbols which may be found in any textbook on genetics.

In addition to a history of definite psychosis or nervous disease, it is desirable to secure evidence of the various less direct and specific factors which throw light on the social reactions and intellectual development as well as the physical make-up and defects of the different members of the family. Because of the possible influence on the patient's health and personality development we wish to know in what kind of a family he was brought up: Were the members intelligent or dull and shiftless; temperamentally stable or unstable and eccentric; of high or low social standing; in good or poor financial circumstances; dependent on charity or welfare relief.

It is not sufficient to ask simply the general question: has any member of the family been insane or nervous? A great many persons will answer in the negative, whereas, a detailed inquiry will often bring out a number of instances of nervous or mental troubles or personality traits which may have an important influence on the patient. In a similar way questions regarding physical defects and diseases in the ancestors must be as specific as possible. All questions should be put in non-technical terms, and judgment and discrimination must be used in accepting as a settled fact diagnoses or causes of death as given by the informant. A descriptive statement as a rule is preferable to a one-word diagnosis.

Specific inquiry should be made concerning each member of the family indicated below and the data recorded in the sequence given. Emphasis should be laid in the inquiry on facts regarding the members of the family *who have been in close contact with the patient* because of their possible influence on his mental development and attitudes, his success or failure, and on the development of his personality disorder or mental breakdown. A grandmother or aunt because of her bringing up of a child may have had more of an influence than a mother or father who was absent. We wish to know therefore what kind of a person the grandmother or aunt was, her tendencies, her attitude toward people and things, and particularly her attitude toward the patient. These may be much more important than her birthplace, age, civil status and age and cause of death, which, however, should be included in the statements to round out the picture of that person. The same principles apply to facts about other members of the family. If the informant has no knowledge regarding any individual of the given generations, it should invariably be mentioned. It is not permissible to say that the family history is negative. Every family has some influence on the development and mental health or illness of its members.

The direct line includes

Paternal grandfather
Paternal grandmother
Maternal grandfather
Maternal grandmother
Father
Mother

Children in family, siblings or brothers and sisters of patient. Record in order of birth, including stillbirths and those dead

Children of patient, give in order of birth

The collateral line includes

Uncles, aunts and cousins

The aim should be to obtain as complete information as possible regarding all members of the direct line and the collateral lines. With this object in view, the history of each individual of the different generations, as above indicated, should be inquired about and the facts recorded in an orderly way. The data may be conveniently arranged and classified as follows:

1. Name, relationship to the patient, living or dead, age, cause of death.

2. Character and disposition—(accomplishments in school and at work; sociable and agreeable or seclusive, distant; calm and easy-going or tense, irritable, worrisome, etc.; aggressive or submissive).

3. Rôle played in family life (with special reference to patient).

4. Psychopathic personality: eccentricity, seclusiveness, emotional instability (exuberant, depressive, cyclothymic), irritability, stubbornness, suspiciousness, nomadism, criminality, sexual perversions, etc. Were these traits habitual or temporary under certain conditions. Describe conditions.

5. Alcoholism, drug addiction, or exposure to other toxic exogenous agents.

6. Psychiatric and neurological disorders:

Mental disorders with or without organic brain disease.

Neurological disorders with or without mental manifestations.

Convulsions in any form.

7. Mental deficiency: idiot, imbecile, moron (congenital or acquired).

8. Physical defects, diseases and anomalies:

Some of these are the following:

(a) *General*

Gastrointestinal.

Cardiovascular, often referred to as "apoplexy," "stroke" or paralysis.

Renal disease.

Cancer.

Gout.

(b) *Infections*

Tuberculosis.

Syphilis.

Other infections: typhoid, rheumatism, pneumonia, etc.

(c) *Endocrine and metabolism disorders*

Giantism, dwarfism.

Obesity, abnormal leanness.

Thyroid disease, diabetes.

(d) *Defects of development and anomalies;* deaf mutism, albinism, congenital deformities, unusually large or small hands, feet, or head.

9. Economic status: Not only because of the possible relationship of economic stress or security to mental stress or mental health, but because of the importance in consideration of the restoration of a patient to his home, it is essential that a detailed account of the economic status of the

family be obtained. Inquiry should be made regarding the income of the members of the family, especially of those responsible for the support of the patient, their occupations, whether regular or seasonal, the type of home, the amount of rent paid, the kind of neighborhood, etc. Changes in the economic status and living conditions, particularly recent ones, should be inquired into. If the family has received relief from private or public agencies the dates of such relief and the names and addresses of these agencies should be ascertained.

d. Personal History:

It is especially desirable and helpful to gain full details with regard to the reaction that the patient showed towards the various experiences through which he passed. Much of importance in the story given by the patient may be "read between the lines." The manner in which he expresses himself indicates level of intelligence, degree of education. Choice of word or phrase, restraint or lack of it, flow of ideas, tone of voice, and so on, all aid in gaining insight into the emotional make-up and nature of the problem. It cannot be overemphasized that there are at least three approaches that should be made with respect to events in the life history of the patient: (1) a detailed account of events or experiences; (2) the patient's attitude towards the events or experiences; (3) the attitude that the parents, guardians and others assumed toward the patient's responses to various situations.

For example, if the patient had measles at the age of eight, it is advisable to know the intensity of the physical disease, but one should also know how the patient reacted in feeling to his illness. Was he essentially indifferent? Was he overanxious? Was he fearful? Did he look for solicitude? Did he "capitalize" his illness for purposes of gaining the interests of others? The attitude of the parents or guardians should be known. Were they neglectful? oversolicitous? reasonably careful? How did they respond to the patient's desires and feelings? Was father's attitude different from that of mother's? If there were older or younger children in the family, how did they act towards the patient's illness?

Obviously it is not feasible to obtain and record *all* the events and reactions in any person's life. For practical purposes we resort to a *sampling* of these events and reactions, the samples having been selected because of their recognized importance in psychiatric syndromes. These samples are indicated in the outline following as guides for inquiry. In persons having mental disorders due to old age, brain disease, infection or accident, the earliest life history and reactions may not be as important for the understanding and treatment of a patient as the more recent events. But for a large number of psychiatric disorders which develop on a basis of abnormal personalities, a detailed history of the life development from its beginning is essential for such understanding and treatment. Because of the importance of knowing what the reactions of the person were to events as they occurred in his life, the following outline points out inquiries that should be made regarding these reactions along with the history of events.

The student and physician are advised to study carefully this outline. It should be realized that it is only a guide which may have to be amplified in detail in the individual case in order to obtain a clear picture of the life and experiences and reactions of the person who is a patient.

PERSONAL HISTORY

Age Date and place of birth

1. INFANCY (Birth to fifth year)

    Mother's condition during pregnancy: Occupation during pregnancy; physical injuries or accidents of the mother; use of intoxicants; attitude toward pregnancy; child wanted or unwanted; attempts at abortion; change in disposition; depression, worries, "mental shock," or other emotional aberrations.

Character of labor: Easy or hard; spontaneous or instrumental.

Condition at birth: Full term or premature, developmental defects or deformities; weight, general condition; difficulty in resuscitation; evidence of injury to head or other parts.

Feeding: Breast or bottle fed, and how long; reaction to nursing; reaction to weaning; vomiting; difficulties in eating habits.

Development: Age of sitting up, creeping, walking, talking, and teething; habits of sleep.

Bed-wetting, when stopped; toilet habits, when and how established and reaction to the training.

Growth, slow or rapid; underweight or overweight or average; when growth changes occurred.

Diseases: Inquire specifically about diphtheria, measles, whooping cough, scarlet fever, mumps, meningitis, otitis, pneumonia and record whether absent or present, getting details of age, date of onset, character and severity of illness, names and addresses of hospitals and physicians who treated the child and reaction of the child in illness and convalescence, and final result; attitude of parents towards the child's illness.

Convulsions: If present, get all details as for diseases above. If absent, record this.

Injuries and operations: Details similar to those under the heading "Diseases" with reaction of child.

Disposition: Docile, happy, cranky, peevish, fretful, temper tantrums, (get details particularly as to whether one or more characteristics were constant); did disposition vary with health or environmental changes such as changes in the family group; effect of discordant marital or other domestic relationships in the family.

Attitude toward family: Response to mother, father and siblings (obedient, affectionate, peevish, resentful, fearful, jealous).

Attitude of family toward child: Reasonable, sensible care, neglect, oversolicitude, jealousy on part of older children, with attempts at mistreatment, or mothering by them.

Sex life: Masturbation, age first noticed, reaction of child and of parents, and method of management.

Neurotic manifestations and habit disturbances: Thumb sucking, night terrors, phobias, tics, speech difficulties.

2. CHILDHOOD (Fifth year to puberty)

Diseases, operations and injuries: Inquire and record here as for infancy with reactions of child.

Habits: Of sleep (regular or irregular, fitful, sleep walking); of eating (regular or irregular, "fussy," food likes and dislikes); of dressing (dependent on or independent of assistance, interest in appearance, untidy or clean); of toilet (regular or irregular, casual or ceremonial, attitude of mother toward use of cathartics or enemas).

Disposition: Cheerful, happy, cranky, irritable, sulky.

School history: Age at beginning, type of school, progress in grades, interest in studies; reaction to school; behavior in school toward teachers and classmates.

Attitude toward playmates: What were his play preferences; shy, bashful, timid, sociable or seclusive; did he lead or follow others.

Attitude toward family: Affectionate, demonstrative, cold, distant, restrained toward parents and siblings; jealousy of siblings.

Sex life: Masturbation, age first noticed, reaction of child and of parents and method of management.

Curiosity: questions about birth, marriage, etc., information given and reaction of child; sex activities with boys or girls and attitude of parents and management by them; reaction of child.

Neurotic traits: Mannerisms, tics, stuttering, bed-wetting, phobias, night terrors, vomiting, etc.

Religious training and interests: Family religious affiliation and training of child; reaction of child to this; opportunities in the home for esthetic culture.

Output of energy: Slow, sluggish, inactive or energetic, active or overactive; were these traits constant or did they appear periodically; if the latter, under what circumstances.

Institutional life: If reared or trained in an institution during the developmental period, give description in detail including the reactions to any opportunities for training.

3. ADOLESCENCE (Beginning at puberty)

Age at puberty: In girls, previous information regarding menstruation and reaction to first period.

School history: Progress—same, faster or slower than in childhood; interest increased or decreased; attitudes toward schoolmates and teachers, men and women; grade reached; and age at leaving school and cause of leaving.

Occupation: Age at which begun, kinds of work obtained on initiative of self or others, exact dates and places of employment, wages received, interest shown in work, attitude toward employers and co-workers, reasons for changes, success or failure in positions, economic status (self-supporting or dependent on family or others); use made of wages.

Physical constitution: Strong, robust, average, sickly, frail; average weight, underweight, overweight; rate of growth.

Diseases, operations and injuries: Get details as indicated for these in *Infancy.*

Disposition: Same as in childhood, or was change noticed, if so, was change related to any external event (inquire carefully); early addiction to alcohol; if sent to an institution during adolescence, note adaptation to institutional life and, in legal cases, the effect of coming into the hands of the law, reactions to sentence, incarceration, and probation.

Attitude toward family: Same as in childhood or changed, and, if so, in what way and toward what member of family (e. g., continued compliance and submissiveness or development of independence and resentment of advice); share plans or ideas; was one particular member of family a confidant; quarrel with siblings.

Interests and social activities: Describe in detail how patient spent his free time and what he was interested in, plans for future; recreational facilities in the home or community; companionships.

Sex life: Masturbation (begun, continued, or stopped during this period); reaction to this; interest in sex literature; frank and open or constrained about sex; extent of sex information and how obtained; interest in and association with the same and opposite sex; preference shown for associates of same, older, or younger age; inquire particularly about changed attitudes at this period.

Religious training and interests: Were there any changes in *training* at this period; what was reaction; any change in *interest,* if so, what prompted this change.

Output of energy: Describe as under CHILDHOOD noting any change and indicating particularly the goals toward which the energy was mainly directed; development and use of any special talents.

4. ADULT LIFE

Education: Continued in college or other institution; progress; age at leaving and reasons; attitude toward teachers and fellow students; attitude toward improvement; interest in everyday affairs or in the mystical or occult.

Occupation: Places and kind of work, wages received, length of time positions held, reasons for change; attitude toward work, and positions; toward employers and co-workers; success or failure; economic status reached (comfortable, marginal or dependent on family or friends or relief agencies; if the latter, get names and addresses of agencies); if not occupied how supported: begging, stealing, etc.

Attitude toward family: (Parents and siblings.) Continuation or change in family ties and reasons for change; dependence on or independence of family; contributions toward family support; attitude toward parents and siblings and other relatives; harmony or disharmony in family.

Sex life: If single, reasons given for remaining so, attitude toward opposite sex and marriage; if married, description of partner, age, reasons given for marrying, length of courtship or engagement; who took active part in courtship; date and place of marriage; where and with whom lived; character of married life (compatible, harmony or disharmony, jealousy, extramarital attachments or relations); children, dates of birth, attitude of patient toward their coming and their presence.

In women, obtain full details of menstrual history and description of physical and mental reactions to first period and at periods subsequently. Also obtain history of pregnancies, abortions, childbirth, reactions to these or illnesses connected with them; if menopause has been reached record age and symptoms, particularly the mental and physical reaction of patient to it.

Also inquire about sexual relations; frequency, initiative taken by which partner, nature of precautions taken and by which partner; approach to sexual relations and reactions to them; other sexual activities indulged in (fellatio, cunnilingus, or pederasty) and reaction to these; interference with act (premature ejaculation, premature detumescence, withdrawal); other types of substituted sex activity such as peeping or looking, beating, fetishism, exhibitionism.

Diseases, injuries and operations: Get all details and reaction of patient to them and final results.

Disposition: Calm, easygoing or quick-tempered, impulsive, irritable, spells of exuberance or depression, unemotional, apathetic or indifferent (care should be taken to ascertain whether one of these traits was outstanding and comparatively constant or whether the disposition varied under different conditions and what these conditions were).

Attitude toward society: Law abiding (by natural inclination or through real or imagined fear); helpful to others and in what way shown; antagonistic to law and order and how expressed (membership in recalcitrant groups against society as organized; overt antisocial acts; lying, stealing, forgery, extortion, blackmail, homicide, and other criminal acts).

Alcohol: Intemperate, moderate, or total abstainer; if intemperate, age at which drinking began, apparent cause of excesses (economic losses, loss of loved ones, other disappointments), kind of beverage consumed and approximate amounts; periodic or steady drinker, alone or in company of men or women; usual reaction to alcohol; behavior when under influence; did drinking interfere with work.

If intemperate, inquire about attacks of neuritis, delirium, hallucinatory episodes, suspicions, ideas of jealousy.

Other toxic influences: Drug habits, occupational poisons (lead, arsenic, phosphorus, mercury, etc); illuminating gas poisoning, nicotine intoxication, food toxicoses.

5. PREVIOUS ATTACKS OF MENTAL DISORDERS

Get dates, places where treated, apparent causes, duration of attacks and symptomatology and outcome; associated physical diseases.

6. ONSET AND SYMPTOMS OF THE PSYCHIATRIC DISORDER

Often the disorder appears to have gradually developed in connection with causes, physical or mental, or both, operating over a comparatively long period; in some cases the causes may be indefinite or not easily elicited, but careful inquiry should be made in such instances for possible etiologic factors and an evaluation made of them.

In other cases, however, the mental breakdown seems to have come on more or less abruptly as if precipitated by some special occurrence or situation; especially to be inquired about are *Precipitating Causes.*

a. *Mental:* Of an emotional nature such as love affairs, sexual episodes, disappointments, reverses, quarrels, separations, deaths in the family, childbirth, etc.

b. *Physical:* Such as acute or chronic illness, infection, childbirth, exhaustion, injury, operation, etc.

Take as far as possible a spontaneous account beginning with the date when the first symptoms were noticed in the patient. In this connection particular attention should be given to changes in behavior, in mood, in manner of speech, in attitude toward others and toward work.

The early symptoms may be physical. In an organic brain disease we may find among the first symptoms an eye-muscle palsy, a fainting spell, headache, pains, etc.; in constitutional mental disorders the onset may be associated with prominent physical complaints, e. g., gastrointestinal symptoms, fussing about health, hypochondriasis, etc.

Get a detailed description of what feelings the patient expressed, what he talked about and how he acted:

Inquiry should be made regarding the appearance of suspicious, unusual interests, peculiar ideas, delusions or hallucinations in various fields and the reactions to them.

Was there forgetfulness, confusion or delirium.

Always inquire regarding suicidal inclinations or attempts, threats of violence, assaults or homicidal tendencies.

Compare statements made by different persons and try to evaluate conflicting statements to arrive at the truth.

What treatment was given at home; names and addresses of physicians in attendance.

What led to the patient's being taken to a hospital or coming to a clinic.

Date on which patient was taken from home to hospital; by what means taken, by whom accompanied, and what was the patient's reaction to the removal.

THE PERSONALITY

(Synopsis)

I. General Intelligence, Knowledge and Judgment

II. Output of Energy—Activity Levels

III. General Attitude Toward Human Environment

IV. Attitude Toward Self: Other Character Traits

V. Special Personal Attitudes, Interests and Adaptations

VI. Emotional Reactions

VII. Sexual Tendencies and Adjustments

VIII. Summary of Personality Traits

III

SURVEY OF THE PRESENTING FEATURES OF THE PERSONALITY

The following outline for obtaining information on the personality organization, while not as elaborate and detailed as may be found in some of the larger works devoted to the subject, is sufficient for a fairly comprehensive survey of the individual's reaction patterns if used skilfully and judiciously by the interviewer. The useful general plan of the previous editions of this book has been followed; however, it was found advisable to make some rearrangements and additions of subtopics and suggestions.

I. *General Intelligence, Knowledge and Judgment*

Learning at school easy or difficult.

Did he keep up with his classes; if not, what was the apparent reason.

Specially smart in certain subjects but deficient in others.

What did the teachers say about it.

Attention and concentration (at school and later).

Memory capacity and characteristics.

Education commensurate with opportunities.

Good observer; logical and orderly in thinking.

Considered to have good common sense.

Capable in positions.

Quick, impulsive or deliberate in judgments.

Capable of giving valuable advice to others.

Definite or vague in personal plans.

Foresight in planning.

Practical; good or bad manager.

Skill in use of tools or mechanical devices.

II. *Output of Energy—Activity Levels*

As a child lively and active at play or work, or sluggish and lazy.

Was imagination lively or not noticeable in play.

Naturally talkative or inclined to be quiet or silent.

Awkward or graceful in speech.

Hard worker, energetic, hustler, or slow, sluggish, deliberate or intermediary.

Temperamental worker.

Work easily blocked by scruples or doubts.

Committed to routine or changes easily.

Energy spent sensibly or in a desultory way.

Recuperative powers from illness or fatigue.

Tendency to overactivity, too much drive or tension.

Overactive or inactive by fits and starts.

Amount of investigatory behavior, originality in procedures.

Interest in athletics, sports and recreations.

History of wandering or hoboing.

III. *General Attitude Toward Human Environment*

Play freely with other children as a child; types of play preferred.

Obedient as a child or difficult to train.

Bashful or ill at ease with strangers.

At social gatherings, the "life of the party" or a "wall-flower."

Sociable, easy to get acquainted, many friends.

Or distant, aloof, preference to be alone; how rationalized.

Selfish or generous, kind-hearted.

Self-sufficient in trouble or eager for contacts and sympathy.

Tactless, fault-finding, quarrelsome, able to cooperate and work with others, or not.

Genuine respect for the rights of others.

Inclined to criticize others.

Allow personal mistakes to be pointed out.

Stubborn and insistent about having own way.

Resistant to advice or suggestible and dependent on the opinions of others.

Trustful or suspicious, holding grudges.

Jealous or envious of attainments and successes of others

Easily offended, feel slights when none were intended.

Satisfied with personal environment or feels above it.

Particular dissatisfactions.

Adapt easily to new situations (as when away from home, moving to new communities, change of work, and so on).

Any marked differences in behavior in the home and when outside.

General range of interests, wide or narrow.

IV. *Attitude Toward Self: Other Character Traits*

Tendency to reveal much of inner life, personal views, aims, ambitions, mental conflicts, and so on.

Frank and open or reserved, reticent and shut-in.

Tendency to talk, unburden self, or not.

Any inclination to self-pity. Tendency to overemphasize or to disregard aches and pains.

Over-conscientious, particular, finicky and over-scrupulous or slipshod and careless.

Inferiority feelings, tendency to underrate self and abilities.

Tendency to shirk, evade or procrastinate.

Honest and truthful or inclined to lie and deceive.

Egotistical, vain, proud, conceited and given to self-admiration.

Foppish, any unusual attention to dress, or careless in this respect.

Self-reliant, a leader or a follower.

Self-assertive or submissive.

Courageous or cowardly.

Affectionate, demonstrative or cold.

Many, few or no friends.

Attracted by what qualities in others.

Family attachments strong or weak.

Marked fondness or antagonism for any member of family (father, mother, sibling or other relative).

Any marked change in family ties between childhood and adult life.

V. *Special Personal Attitudes, Interests and Adaptations*

How well adapted to reality.

"Matter of fact" or unimaginative.

Or over-imaginative, visionary, daydreaming and inclined to build air castles.

Absent-minded, tendency to preoccupation.

Greatest satisfaction gained from present work or from other pursuits.

Ambitious and in what direction; extent of urge toward fame, and to what extent has the urge been satisfied.

If deformed or physically ugly, how compensated.

Interest in new experiences.

Interest in public life, politics, philanthropy, social work or reformation; any opinions rebelling against social law or order, revolutionary ideas.

Extent and character of reading habits.

Interest and activities in art, music and the drama.

Interest in science and natural phenomena.

Comfort gained from religion, or interest superficial; regular or occasional church attendance.

Superstitious.

Vague gropings such as spiritualism, occult studies, or interest in odd cults.

Active spender and show-off with money, or miserly and close.

Types of hobbies and fads.

Interest in sports or other diversions.

Gambling or betting habits.

Any converted tendencies such as recklessness, speed manias, excesses in dress or other personal habits; creation of exciting situations, etc.

Alcoholic habits; abstainer, moderate drinker, heavy drinker or solitary drinker.

VI. *Emotional Reactions*

Placid, eventempered or phlegmatic.

Cheerful, light-hearted, optimistic.

Or gloomy, pessimistic and worrisome, looking on the dark side of things.

Irritable, impulsive, easily angered, tantrums and explosive outbursts.

Changeability of mood, periods of buoyancy or despondency.

Good sense of humor or inadequate in this respect.

Tendency to brooding without apparent reason, or on certain topics.

Easily frightened, under what special circumstances.

Tendency to apprehensiveness and forebodings.

Sensitive, touchy, grumbling or fault-finding.

Reactions to failures, disappointments, business troubles, responsibility, deaths of relatives or friends.

Crave sympathy in trouble, seem to enjoy discomforts.

Any resemblance to other members of the family in above characteristics.

VII. *Sexual Tendencies and Adjustments*

Frank or secretive about sexual matters.

Amount and accuracy of sex information possessed.

Attitude toward opposite sex or own sex.

Tomboy, "mother's boy," mannish or effeminate.

At ease or shy in presence of opposite sex.

Many, few or no love affairs.
Attracted by older or younger persons of opposite sex.
Reactions to disappointments in love.
Reasons for broken love affairs.
Decided or uncertain when confronted with questions of engagement or marriage.
Adaptation to married life.
Attitude toward the partner; affectionate, kind and understanding, or dissatisfied, fault-finding, irritable and jealous, or domineering or submissive.
Attitude toward having children.
In women, fear of pregnancy.
Sexual demands numerous or few.
Adequate potency or psychic impotence, ejaculatio precox, frigidity, and so on.
Masturbation, age at onset, duration and frequency.
Type of conflict, if any.
Perversions: homosexual, sadistic, masochistic or fetishistic; other unsocialized sex habits.
Sexual curiosity, fondness for gossip about sexual matters.
Intolerance of sexual topics and easily disgusted.
Excessive modesty or prudishness.
Special demand for neatness, cleanliness or moralizing.
Idiosyncracies toward food or odors.
Special tendencies to cruelty, "plaguing" or tantalizing others; how received when the "tables are turned."

VIII. *Summary of Personality Traits*

At the conclusion of the inquiry into the make-up, a brief summary of the outstanding tendencies and characteristics should be made, with an attempt to group them into a reaction pattern that will be of use in directing the management, therapy and final adjustment of the person under consideration, and that will also serve the purpose of teaching, conferences and special research studies.

PHYSICAL EXAMINATION

(Synopsis)

INTRODUCTION

I. GENERAL TYPE, APPEARANCE AND CONDITION

II. THORACIC ORGANS

IV. GENITO-URINARY ORGANS

III. DIGESTIVE AND ABDOMINAL ORGANS

V. NERVOUS SYSTEM

1. General and Subjective Sensations
2. Cranial Nerves
3. Cutaneous and Deep Sensibility
4. Vasomotor and Trophic Conditions
5. Motor Functions
6. Reflexes
7. Myopathies
8. Fibrillary Twitchings
9. Tremor
10. Speech
11. Organic Reflexes
12. Convulsions

VI. VEGETATIVE NERVOUS SYSTEM

VII. ENDOCRINE GLANDS

VIII. SUMMARY OF PHYSICAL EXAMINATION

IV

PHYSICAL EXAMINATION

Introduction

It cannot be too strongly emphasized that all psychiatric patients require a careful physical examination. This is obviously necessary for the purpose of determining if the patient is suffering from any injury, physical disease, or impairment of general health and for the purpose of determining if there are present any signs and symptoms which are characteristic of certain types of mental disorder. The correct diagnosis and management will in many cases depend largely on the physical findings, particularly in mental conditions due to disease of the nervous system. Moreover, because of the possible relationship of physical constitution to type of mental disorder, a complete description of the physique and indication of the type of body build are of importance in the clinical study.

Some of the most common and also the most serious mistakes which physicians make are due to their failure to discover and correctly interpret significant physical signs and symptoms in the early stages of various mental disorders.

The lack of cooperation and even opposition to examination which mental patients often exhibit make the task of the physician doubly difficult and not infrequently tax severely his resourcefulness and patience. The method of approach and the technique of examination are, therefore, extremely important matters if satisfactory results are to be obtained from the physical examination of mental patients.

Because of lack of cooperation or resistiveness, a complete examination may not be possible upon one attempt but few patients are continuously unapproachable and repeated attempts should be made until the facts of the physical condition are obtained. Doubtful findings should be checked by repeated examinations until the physician is assured of the true facts.

The following physical examination guide presents in condensed form the requirements for a fairly thorough examination of the various organs and functions. In some cases additional tests and further investigations will be necessary to clear up complex or obscure conditions. Routine urine and blood examinations, including a blood Wassermann, are indicated in all cases. Special indications may call for a spinal fluid Wassermann, cell count, protein content, colloidal gold reaction, and pressure studies. The indications in brain diseases and other somatic states for basal metabolism tests, blood chemistry, roentgenograms, electroencephalograms, cardiograms, tests for exogenous toxic substances, kidney function, and so on, must always be kept in mind.

PHYSICAL EXAMINATION

I. General Type, Appearance and Condition

a. *General Appearance*

Condition of clothes.

Posture.

Type of facial expression.

Color of hair and eyes.

Station and gait.

Speech defects.

b. *Anthropological Make-up*

1. Height. Weight (present).
2. Malformations and asymmetries: skull, face, ears, palate, body, spine, thorax, pelvis, hands, feet, sexual organs.
3. Osseous system: general stature, frame, and skeletal type. Abnormalities in height, size of head, face, and jaw bones, setting of teeth.

   Disproportion between size of extremities and trunk. Torso-leg ratio (the trunk length is the distance in inches between the suprasternal notch and the anterior superior spine of the ilium. The leg length is the distance in inches between the anterior superior spine of the ilium and the internal malleolus. In a properly proportioned person the leg length is twice the trunk length (torso-leg-ratio).)
4. Body type: asthenic, pyknic, athletic, dysplastic, undetermined. Unusual fat distributions.

c. *Nutrition*

1. Poor, fair, good, obese.
2. Usual weight: subcutaneous fat, amount and distribution.
3. Muscles: tone and size.

d. *Skin, Hair, and Nails*

1. Color and texture of skin, general complexion.
2. Anaemia, jaundice, bronzing, dropsy, pallor, flushing, cyanosis, eruptions, trophic disorders, perspiration: amount and distribution.
3. Hair: color, quantity, texture, unusual distribution.
4. Nails: appearance and condition, smooth, rough, fissured, brittle.

e. *Glandular System*

1. Lymphatic: axillary, epitrochlear, and inguinal lymph nodes, salivary, thyroid, thymus, mammary glands.

f. *Mouth, Teeth, and Naso-Pharynx*

1. Mucous membranes, tongue, gums, fetor, pyorrhoea.
2. Teeth: condition and number missing.
3. Tonsils and adenoids.
4. Naso-pharynx.

g. *Acute or Chronic Diseases*

1. Temperature, pulse, and respiration.
2. Scars, bruises, hernias, and injuries (to be carefully noted and fully described).
3. New growths (examine carefully for epitheliomata, and breast tumor).
4. Evidence of syphilis: scars, mucous patches, glands, tibial crests and exostoses of skull. Date of infection, how treated.
5. Signs of gout, rheumatism or tuberculosis (other than respiratory).
6. Acute infections, local or general signs.

II. Thoracic Organs

1. *Circulatory Organs:* Is there any palpitation In attacks Due to what Subjective sensation of arhythmia Dyspnoea Oedema Any attacks of pain or anxiety.

Heart: The impulse seen and felt in what area Relative dullness (right, upper and left borders) Give *measurement from median line,* beside the statement as to nipple-line; in pathological cases draw a chart.

Sounds and bruits (localized): Pay special attention to muffling of the first sound, to duplication; to change of murmurs on inspiration and by position and to rhythm and accentuation Take electrocardiogram when indicated.

Radial pulse: Rate, quality on lying and sitting and standing Special attention to variability, through position or emotion or exertion, effect of moderate exercise.

Condition of vessels: Radial, brachial and temporal arteries Arcus senilis Sclerosis of veins Varicosities Pulsations of neck.

Blood pressure: Systolic and diastolic, lying and sitting (repeat later in the examination).

2. *Respiratory Organs:* Is there any difficulty of breathing, permanent or in attacks Any pain on deep inspiration Any cough or expectoration History of hemorrhage Naso-pharynx obstruction or other abnormalities Larynx, hoarseness or other symptoms.

Shape and elasticity of chest: Expansion, frequency of respiration Respiratory movements (compare both sides in deep inspiration and expiration).

Lungs: Palpitation, percussion, auscultation.

III. Digestive and Abdominal Organs

Appetite: Thirst, anorexia, nausea; relation to quantity and quality of food Vomiting (time and form); eruptions and brashes; pain (locality, irradiation and time).

Abdomen: Flat, soft, distended, pain, tenderness, rigidity, retraction.

Abdominal organs: Stomach and liver outlines; gall bladder; spleen; floating kidney.

Digestion: Movements of bowels Any subjective feeling of obstacles Form of stools Flatulence and distention Constipation, hemorrhoids and fistulas.

IV. Genito-Urinary Organs

Micturition: Frequency, nocturnal, diurnal, subjective complaints Urine Laboratory examination.

In women: Menstruation (regularity and type; duration and amount and probable cause of abnormalities); accompanying symptoms (pains and especially nervous symptoms) Evidence of menopause.

Discharge; constant, profuse, color (smears).

Gynecological examination: findings, their history and possible relation to the rest of the status.

In men: Penis development, scars, ulcers, discharge (smears) phimosis.

Testicle—descended or undescended, size, consistency Varicocele, hydrocele.

Prostate—size and consistency.

V. Nervous System

1. *General and Subjective Sensations*

General feeling of well-being or exhaustion, general complaints, weakness, etc.

Vertigo: Constant, occasional, or occurring on definite changes of position, when the patient walks or in the dark.

Headache: Whole head or limited space; frontal, vertical, bi-temporal, occipital, constant, or periodic, aggravated at night or by some special cause, as with heat; with or without tenderness of head or spine to touch or pressure.

Pains: Ovarian, infra-mammary, lumbar and vertex pains (in hysteria).

Neuralgic pains, 5th nerve, intercostal nerves, sciatic nerve, with pain points, etc., and muscular pains.

General or wandering pains: Precordial pains with or without anxiety Sudden shooting pains.

Pains in bones, afternoon or night.

Girdle pains: Zones of hyperesthesia (See section 3).

2. *Cranial Nerves*

1*st Nerve:* Smell Anosmia, paranosmia Test each nostril separately with the standard test substances.

2*nd Nerve:* Vision Acuity, dimness, limitation of field, scotoma, hemianopsia, color sense Corneal scars Cataract Ophthalmoscopic examination.

3*rd,* 4*th and* 6*th Nerves:* (Eyelids, muscles and pupils) Test for ptosis, nystagmus, ocular palsies, squint, double vision, convergence, exophthalmos, enophthalmos, size of palpebral fissures.

Pupils: Size, shape, outlines, adhesions of iris, inequality of pupils Reaction to light and in accommodation; consensual, sympathetic, and psycho-reflexes.

5*th Nerve:* (Motor portion) muscles of mastication, masseters, temporals, and pterygoids (sensory portion), face and anterior scalp, conjunctiva, mucous membranes, sensitivity of supraorbital and infraorbital exits.

Taste: Anterior 2/3 tongue (see 9th N.).

Neuralgia or facial pains in distribution of nerve should be inquired for.

7*th Nerve:* Muscles of forehead, face, mouth and orbicularis oculi: do they act symmetrically, can patient whistle.

8*th Nerve:* Hearing (cochlear portion) test acuity of hearing Differentiate central, peripheral, and functional deafness Tinnitus and ear noises Unilateral hallucinations of hearing may correspond to diseased ear; (vestibular portion) equilibrium, vertigo.

Otoscopic examination: External canal and drum.

9th Nerve: Deglutition and sensation back of tongue and upper pharynx.

Taste: (together with 5th nerve) Test separately anterior 2/3 supplied by 5th N. and posterior 1/3 supplied by 9th N.

10*th Nerve:* Test muscles of soft palate and larynx Note disturbances in phonation, respiration and heart action Laryngoscopic examination if indicated.

11*th Nerve:* Test action of sterno-mastoid and trapezius muscles Position and movements of the head and scapulae.

12*th Nerve:* Muscles of tongue Position of protruded tongue and other movements, atrophy and tremor.

3. *Cutaneous and Deep Sensibility:* (A few tests of localization of touch and pain sensations obligatory to exclude hysteria; in all cases with subjective complaints or where any indication and doubt exists, complete examination is advised).

Subjective complaints: (Formication, feeling of needles and pins, numbness).

Tactile sensibility: (Use the finger tip, cotton, or pin) Compare both sides of face, arms, hands, fingers, breasts, inner and outer aspects of thighs and legs.

Never omit the ulnar side and the area outside and above the knee, the sole and dorsum of foot and in hysteria the breast and other points of predilection of hysterical anaesthesia.

Localization of touch (time and space) and tickle.

Sensibility to pain: (Cautious pricks with a pin, localization in time and space), with or without the attention of the patient.

Sensations of heat and cold: (Cold water and warm water in a glass tube) Pain and temperature sense may be lost without any other sensory disorder in syringomyelia and in lesions of the lateral columns of the cord, and rarely in hysteria. These disorders may occur without any other sensory defect.

Vibratory sense

Stereognostic sense: Does the patient recognize two or three dimensions, and objects from mere palpation with the eyes closed—of special importance for the study of disturbances of sensory elaboration.

Sense of position: Best studied with the motor functions.

Tenderness of nerve trunks and muscles on pressure and percussion: The distributions to be noted on the drawings of the body surface.

Analgesia of the ulnar nerve (Biernacki's sign); anaesthesia of eye-ball, of testicles.

4. *Vasomotor and Trophic Conditions*

Salivation, seborrhoea.

Cyanosis or pallor; scaliness or glossy appearance of skin; loss of hair; change of nails.

Blushing, dermatographia General and localized perspiration.

Temperature of paralyzed or anaesthetic parts.

5. *Motor Functions*

Right- or left-handed.

Any paresis or paralysis apparent or established by testing the functions of successive segments.

Motility of facial muscles (wrinkle forehead, close eyes tightly, show teeth, purse lips, whistle) and movements of jaw, tongue, palate, etc. (See under Cranial Nerves) Test strength of muscles of neck, shoulder girdle, trunk and extremities.

Upper limbs: Compare hand grips, strength of flexors, extensors and rotators.

Lower limbs: Rise on toes, elevate toes, flex and extend feet, legs and thighs Elevate both legs from bed and hold to fatigue limit—weaker limb sinks first.

Gait: Observe walking, turning, stopping and starting Note limping, shuffling, straddling, stamping, ataxia, steppage, propulsive tendencies, etc.

Coordination: Paralyses and spasticities, writing, buttoning coat and picking up objects Finger-nose, finger-finger and heel-knee tests.

Balancing: Walk straight line; stand with eyes closed, heels and toes together (Romberg position); steady, sways or falls.

Muscle sense: Discrimination of differences in weight; with eyes closed tell the position of limbs; appreciation of passive movements, show by one side the positiou of the limb of the other side.

6. *Reflexes*

(a) *Deep reflexes:* Masseteric; elbow, wrist, thumb, and knee jerk; latter with or without reinforcement, with clonus, or contralateral abductor reflex; knee cap reflex (tapping the finger which pulls down the patella in the lying position, usually giving a better idea of differences of the two sides) Ankle clonus (one or several catches, or a continuous clonus); Achilles tendon reflex.

(b) *Superficial reflexes:* Plantar (with full description as to the Babinski reflex), gluteal, cremasteric, abdominal, epigastric, scapular, corneal, palmar, pharyngeal, sneezing Sexual reflexes (see under 11).

7. *Myopathies*

Examine carefully weak muscles, or those not responding in reflexes: firm and of good tone, or flaccid or deficient in tone, or rigid and contracted Note attitude of limb and the limitation of the motion, active and passive, in every joint.

Atrophy Hypertrophy.

Electrical reaction when indicated of nerve and muscle; mechanical irritability.

8. *Fibrillary Twitchings*

Describe and give distribution.

9. *Tremor*

Of what parts, face, tongue, fingers, etc. Describe as to rhythm, intensity, rapidity.

Condition at rest, during sleep; when first observed.

Condition during motion, how influenced by will.

A sample of writing should always be obtained and inserted in the history, (name, date and test phrase).

10. *Speech*

Note any defect in ordinary conversation.

Speech tests are to be tried in every case (third riding artillery brigade; particular popularity; electricity; Methodist Episcopal; army reorganization; truly rural).

11. *Organic Reflexes and Their Control*

Bladder: Delay of micturition Dribbling from empty bladder, from distended bladder Peculiar sensations on micturition.

Sexual reflexes: Involuntary erection and ejaculation.

Defecation: Is the patient conscious of evacuations.

12. *Convulsions*

Duration and frequency: Occurring night or day, or in early morning Initial cry, scream or other symptoms Extend over head, trunk and extremities, or one side or one member.

Character: Which parts first and most attacked and how do the waves of the tonic and clonic spasm spread What movements predominate Is a paralyzed part omitted or involved.

Observe breathing; pupils; vasomotor conditions; whether there is frothing and biting or talking during attack Relaxation of sphincters.

Consciousness: Totally or partially lost.

Aura: Character, location and spread.

Equivalents with or without what automatic movements.

Psychical and nervous symptoms before and after attack.

Vomiting, headache, sleep, coma.

The presence of convulsions of any type indicates a special examination by electroencephalography when the apparatus and trained personnel are available.

VI. The Vegetative Nervous System

Supplies the involuntary or smooth muscle organs. Evidence of disturbances in function may have been observed in the preceding examination of the voluntary nervous system and viscera. It is advisable, however, to call attention here to some of the more striking signs and symptoms which are considered to indicate alteration of function of the vegetative nervous system. Among these are:

(a) *Sympathetic Division:* Signs of overactivity are warm, dry skin; wide pupils; rapid heart; hypersensitiveness to adrenalin (a sympathetic stimulant).

Cervical Sympathetic: Paralysis gives characteristic symptoms; drooping of lid without loss of voluntary control; small pupil, not dilating when shaded, but contracting to light; enophthalmos, with narrowing of fissure; loss of cilio-spinal (sympathetic) reflex; failure of pupil to dilate under cocaine.

(b) *Autonomic Division:* Signs of overactivity are cool, pale, moist skin; small pupils; slow heart; gastric hyperacidity; sluggish bowel action; hypersensitiveness to pilocarpine (a vagus stimulant).

VII. Endocrine Glands

Evidence of disturbances may have been found and recorded under other headings. But such evidence may be brought together at this place to focus attention on important symptom-complexes. The special guide for the study of endocrine disorders should be used in those cases in which special investigation of the body development and endocrine system is undertaken.

Thyroid

(a) *Hyperthyroidism:* Tachycardia; tremor; perspiration; gastrointestinal overactivity; eye symptoms; excessive reaction to adrenalin (Goetsch test); low carbohydrate tolerance.

(b) *Hypothyroidism:* (1) Myxedematous type shows bradycardia; skin, hair and nail changes; gastrointestinal sluggishness; high carbohydrate tolerance; diminished reaction to adrenalin. (2) Cretin type shows mental and physical deficiency with symptoms of myxedema.

Pituitary

(a) *Hyperfunction:* Onset after puberty gives acromegalic type; enlargement of bones; thickened mucous membranes; enlarged tongue; muscular atrophies; superabundant hair; alteration in sexual functions; reduced carbohydrate tolerance.

Onset before maturity gives giant type; increased length of bone; precocious development of sexual instinct and organs of reproduction.

(b) *Hypofunction:* (Frœhlich's Syndrome) with obesity; general deficiency of hair; infantile sexual organs; short stature; increased carbohydrate tolerance.

Testicle

Hypofunction: Eunuch type shows absence of testicle; obesity; feminine hair distribution; lack of development of external genitalia.

Eunuchoid type shows deficiency of secretion; essentially same signs as in eunuch.

Ovary

Hypofunction: Delayed puberty; infantile uterus; delayed or disordered menstruation; obesity.

Adrenal

(a) *Hyperfunction:* (?) increased blood pressure; low carbohydrate tolerance; glycosuria.

(b) *Hypofunction:* Skin pigmentation; low blood pressure; asthenia (Addison's Syndrome).

Status Lymphaticus: (Related to thymus or adrenal?) Slender frame; feminine contour; feminine hair distribution; smooth skin; hyperplasia of lymphatic system.

VIII. Summary of Physical Examination

The physical findings are to be summarized not merely in the order of examination but especially in order of importance or evolution and in differential diagnosis. Symptoms which make up a characteristic symptom-complex should be grouped together in the summary. Attention should be called to points for further investigation.

Indications for treatment should be added.

Within recent years attention has been called to the correlations between body build, temperament and psychiatric disorders. This point of view became available to psychiatrists particularly through the efforts of Kretschmer, who described the four principal body builds, namely: asthenic, athletic, pyknic and dysplastic. The following table from Kretschmer (Physique and Character. E. Kretschmer. Translated by W. J. H. Sprott. Harcourt, Brace & Co., Inc., New York, 1925) summarizes the correlation of habitus and psychiatric reaction.

Habitus	Schizophrenia Per cent	Manic-depressive psychosis Per cent
Pyknic	2.8	84.6
Asthenic	46.2	4.7
Athletic	17.7	3.5
Dysplastic	19.4	0.0
Unclassified	13.7	7.0

The principal characteristics of the different body types are as follows. The *asthenic* exhibits a deficiency in thickness combined with an average unlessened length. The deficiency is uniform over the entire body—face, neck, trunk, extremities and all the tissues (skin, fat, muscle, bone and vascular apparatus). The individual is lean, narrowly built; the face is long and narrow; it is a shortened egg-shaped face; the profile is angular. The shoulders are narrow; arms and legs are long and lean; the bones of the hands are delicate; the chest is long, narrow and flat; the rib-angle is sharp; abdomen is thin and devoid of fat. The body weight lags behind the body length; the chest measurement lags behind the hip measurement. The skin and soft parts are thin, pale and poor in fat. The hair on the head is thick and spreading. When baldness supervenes it is patchy. The secondary hair growth, on the contrary, is underdeveloped. The beard is fine and uneven; pubic hair is apt to be scanty and the hair on the trunk is still scantier.

The asthenic habitus was found in 46.2 per cent of schizophrenic patients and in 4.7 per cent of manic-depressive patients.

The *athletic* type is a middle-sized to tall man, with wide projecting shoulders, large ("superb") chest, firm abdomen, tapering trunk, "magnificent" legs. The whole development is one of strength. The musculature is strong, sometimes giving the appearance of hypertrophy. The face is commonly of the steep egg-shaped type. The skin shares the general hypertrophy; it is firm and elastic; fat is moderately developed. Sometimes the skin of the face is pasty and puffy and has pimples.

The athletic habitus was observed in 17.7 per cent of the schizophrenic patients and in 3.5 per cent of the manic-depressive group.

The *pyknic* habitus is characterized by pronounced peripheral development of the body cavities. Individuals with this build are of middle height and have a rounded figure; the face is broad and is five-cornered in shape; the large skull is round, broad and deep, but not very high; the limbs are soft, rounded and show little bone or muscle relief; the hands are soft, short and wide; the shoulders are rounded, high and pushed forward. The neck is short and thick; chest circumference is large; the abdomen is large. Obesity is moderate and is specially found in the trunk (fat belly); the fat over other parts of the body is diffuse. The skin is smooth, well-fitting and of moderate thickness. Muscles are soft and of moderate strength. The weight of the body is heavy.

The hair on the head is soft; the hair line recedes. The tendency to baldness is far greater in the pyknic habitus than in the asthenic. The beard is evenly distributed and the axillary and pubic hair is well developed; the hair on the trunk varies from moderate to plenty.

The pyknic habitus was found to dominate in the manic-depressive group of patients; 84.6 per cent with that clinical diagnosis possessed the pyknic habitus.

The fourth or *dysplastic* habitus is generally determined by disorders of the glands of internal secretion. There are three general groups: (a) elongated eunuchoids; (b) eunuchoid and polyglandular fat abnormalities; and (c) infantilism and hypoplasia.

The characteristics of the elongated eunuchoid are great length of extremities in relation to height of body, obliteration of sexual characteristics in the proportion of the trunk (i. e., the asexual pelvis) and well-developed primary (head) hair with scanty secondary hair. There is a smaller subgroup in which the towering skull, high and firm lower jaw and brush-like beard are outstanding. Among women with schizophrenia there is a tendency to masculinity.

Other patients in the dysplastic group exhibit several deviations. There are some patients whose body structure seems to be the result of polyglandular dysfunction. Finally, there is infantilism and types with hypoplasia. There is, for instance, the type of hypoplastic face; acromicria, with an elective hypoplasia of the limbs; a third type of hypoplasia affects the trunk principally.

The dysplastic habitus was not found at all in the manic-depressive group and appeared in 19.4 per cent of the schizophrenic patients.

Finally, Kretschmer was unable to classify the body build in 13.7 per cent of schizophrenic cases and in 7.0 per cent of the manic-depressive group.

Kretschmer concludes that "physique and psychosis do not stand in a direct clinical relation to one another. The physique is not a symptom of the psychosis, but, physique and psychosis, bodily function, and internal diseases, healthy personality and heredity are each, separately, part-symptoms of the constitutional basis which lies at the bottom of the whole."*

Following Kretschmer, other investigators have carried on similar studies. In general, conclusions are that Kretschmer's formulations add a valuable and often a practical viewpoint in the study of clinical psychiatry.

*The above description of Kretschmer's findings is taken from Hinsie: SYLLABUS OF PSYCHIATRY.

MENTAL EXAMINATION

(Synopsis)

Introduction

I. Attitude and General Behavior

II. Attitude and Behavior During Interview

III. Stream of Mental Activity

IV. Emotional Reactions

V. Mental Trend: Content of Thought

VI. Sensorium, Mental Grasp and Capacity

a. Orientation

b. Data of Personal Identification: Remote Memory

c. Memory of Recent Past

d. Retention and Immediate Recall

e. Counting and Calculation

f. Reading

g. Writing

h. School and General Knowledge

i. Intelligence Rating

j. Other Special Mental Functions

k. Insight and Judgment

VII. Summary of Mental Examination

V

MENTAL EXAMINATION

Introduction

The first principle in the examination of patients with mental disorders is to observe carefully and accurately and to record the facts for ourselves and others so that they can be used in an evaluation of symptoms for diagnosis, prognosis, and treatment. In descriptions we should aim for unequivocal statements, and learn to avoid all terms which are open to confusion; wherever there is doubt about terms, it is best to resort to a plain statement of events in simple, non-technical language. This does not prevent the judicious use of all available knowledge, but it does keep one from getting involved in a terminology which is often deceptive and tends to lead to the belief that more is known about the case than the actual facts warrant.

It is important to know what a patient does and says, but before the significance of what he does and says can be evaluated, it is necessary to know from the patient his explanation. It is also important to note what the patients neglect to say. Both a deviant response and complete absence of response to certain questions are important. The examiner is not to interpret actions of a patient from his own standpoint. He is to get the explanation from the patient if possible. It is also important to describe the circumstances under which things are said and done, that is, the setting in which they appear. Hence the important rule in recording clinical observations, that wherever there is anything to be demonstrated, it is necessary to give all available facts. For clarity it may at times be desirable to report conversations in *question and answer* form. This does not mean that the entire examination is to be reported in this way, a procedure very rarely necessary. Records are often overloaded with questions and answers. On the other hand, many records are almost valueless because they give chiefly the examiner's impressions and judgments without recording sufficient facts on which the conclusions are based. It is especially desirable to give in the patient's own words examples of the delusional ideas entertained and the hallucinatory experiences, if any are described. (Such examples also may be valuable in certain cases in relation to medico-legal questions.) The general rule is that the record should contain a sufficiently full report of what the patient actually said and did to permit the reader to form an independent opinion of the case as a whole or of the various reactions shown by the patient.

One must be prepared to spend much time and effort in acquiring a good technique of examination and in learning how to present the facts with proper regard for their psychiatric worth.

In the examination of the patient the physician's mode of approach often determines the attitude of the patient toward the examination. The reserve of the patient is often very great, or if not the reserve, at least the unwillingness to show a clear picture of experience. It is, therefore, neccessary to gain the confidence by treating the patient as a "sensible man or woman." In most cases it is essential to interview the patient privately; the statements may then be obtained freely, often with a feeling of relief to the patient, and distinct gain in the relation between physician and patient.

Any appearance of obnoxious ridicule or dictation or correction or argument on the part of the physician must be avoided. The feelings of the patient, the general situation and the special idiosyncrasies are to be kept in mind above all. Care is necessary to make the patient feel that all is done in a spirit of helpfulness. The aim should be the establishment of a comfortable and wholesome relation of patient to physician.

Physicians often make the mistake of waiting for a disturbed, delirious or negativistic patient to become quiet and freely accessible before undertaking the investigation of the mental condition. It is, however, just as necessary to proceed with the examination of an excited, delirious, or stuporous patient as it is with a quiet or cooperative one. The examination must of course be shaped according to the condition of the patient, but *a good record of the reactions, moods, utterances, etc., during the stormy or non-cooperative period of the psychosis is of the utmost importance.* In fact, it is just these pathological reactions that require the most painstaking study and description. It is, therefore, inexcusable to adopt the plan of waiting for the disappearance of such symptoms before attempting to make an examination.

For purposes of order and systematic approach it becomes necessary to adopt some general plan of work and to arrange observations under certain topical headings. These are selected because they cover the most important manifestations of mental disorder and have a value in differential diagnosis. The order of arrangement suggested in this guide is not necessarily best followed in every case. One must be governed by the condition of the patient and the examination, as mentioned above, must of course be shaped according to the type of disturbance under investigation. The experienced physician stresses that part of the examination which obviously deals with the most important aspects of the case before him.

It is advised that in recording the results of the examination under each division of the guide, use be made of short, concise, summarizing headings, in capitals, in order to indicate and emphasize what the important findings are in each one of the various subdivisions.

I. Attitude and General Behavior

There should be a brief description of what the nurses, physicians and others in contact with the patient observe in the patient. This includes the general behavior of the patient in the situation in which he finds himself.

The general description should cover the following points:

1. *General health and appearance*

   Is the patient sick, weak or strong and healthy. If sick, is most of waking time spent in bed, or up.

   Does patient appear older than his chronological age (prematurely aged), average or younger (immature appearance).

2. *General habits of dress*

   Dresses with extreme care, normal care and neatness, or with utter carelessness. Selects and wears clothes (cosmetics) in peculiar fashion, average or careless fashion.

3. *Personal habits*

   Extremely meticulous and fussy, normal personal habits, extremely slovenly and untidy.

   Keeps room spotlessly clean in a compulsive way, normally clean, untidy.

   Toilet habits; eating habits.

4. *General mood*

   Elated, excited, calm, apathetic, depressed.

5. *Use of leisure*

   Working, reading, conversing or in idleness.

6. *Sociability*

   Extremely gregarious, normally so, seclusive. Has patient made friends in the ward.

7. *Speech*

   Garrulous, normally spontaneous, taciturn, mute. Lisping, stammering, slurring.

   Topics of conversation: Current events, personal troubles, etc.

It is best to write or dictate this division of the mental status at the conclusion of the examination for the reason that the "Attitude and General Behavior" should include a description of what is observed *during the interview,* particularly in reference to the following:

II. Attitude and Behavior During Interview

1. *Attitude toward interviewer*

   Extremely attentive and cooperative, moderately so, or non-cooperative.

2. *Expressive movements*

   Manner—stilted and stereotyped, normally poised or uncontrolled.

   Voice—faint, normal, overloud.

   Posture—stiff, normally relaxed, completely relaxed.

3. *Facial expression*

   a. Pain and grief

      Anxiety, tearfulness, suffering, ironed-out (mask-like), sadness, sorrow, gloominess and hopelessness.

   b. Fear and amazement

      Terror, fear, tenseness, distrust, bewilderment.

   c. Anger

      Anger, irritability, rage, defiance, frowning.

   d. Disgust

      Sulkiness, haughtiness, sneering, conceit, resentment, contempt.

   e. Pleasure and exaltation

      Exalted spirits, ecstasy, beatitude, dreaminess, cheerfulness, happiness, smiling and laughing.

   f. Attention and interest

      Absorption, perplexity, apathy, indifference.

   g. Changeability of mood as exhibited by inconstancy of facial expression.

      Flightiness of mood, steadiness of mood.

4. *Motor activity*

   A description of *motor activity* is important. In case there is hyperactivity, describe a series of motions or acts, giving the sequence of events, as accurately as possible.

a. Walk and gait

Erect, slouching, stooped, swaying, staggering, stiff or awkward.

b. Gestures

Hand movements, tics, twitchings or tremor, picking at himself or clothing, posturing.

c. Motor coordination.

Limpness, rigidity, cog-wheel resistance, waxy flexibility.

d. General activity

Hyperactive, average, underactive, random, spontaneously purposeful, forced, passive movements.

e. Psychomotor retardation

If you suspect psychomotor retardation, determine its presence by giving details such as time required for dressing, carrying out a simple command such as walking across the room, or some other movement.

Examine resistive or non-cooperative patients for negativism, muscular tension, stiffness, catalepsy, suggestibility, automatic obedience, etc. (See Section VII.)

III. Stream of Mental Activity

This is best studied in the patient's spontaneous account or, when this is not given, in the reactions to special questions. This gives an idea of the productivity and of the nature of the stream of thought. Obtain *verbatim* samples of what the patient says.

The patient may exhibit *no disorder* in spontaneous conversation; may answer questions promptly, relevantly and show logical progression in association of ideas.

The patient may be *overproductive* in speech and show volubility, rambling talk, abnormal divertibility, flight of ideas, incoherence, verbigeration or disjointed, scattered utterances. Or with or without overproductivity there may be distractibility of attention, sound associations, peculiar expressions, self-invented words or phrases (neologisms), irrelevancy, echolalia, stereotypy, etc. It should be borne in mind that disturbances in the stream of thought (flight, incoherence, irrelevancy, etc.) may not appear at once or in response to the first few questions. They may appear at some subsequent part of the examination to which reference should be made so that the reader can find the samples. Often disturbances in the stream of thought will be brought out only when the patient's complexes are touched on. Distractibility and flight in elaborations may often be demonstrated by simple tests, such as showing objects, making sounds, speaking certain words and requesting the patient to give a series of associations.

The patient may show a *diminished productivity,* give only an occasional utterance, or there may be a marked slowness in speech with evidence of retardation in the mental processes, or the patient may refuse to speak or to answer any question. In case the patient seems inhibited or retarded, indicate the approximate time to obtain a response, observe whether or not the answer when once started is given rapidly or slowly, with hesitation or pauses.

When the patient is spontaneously productive, record samples of the stream of thought. If the patient says nothing spontaneously, the examiner has to take the initiative and may ask the patient how he likes it where he is, how he is getting on and what the trouble has been that led to his coming to the hospital or clinic. The replies are put down just as they are given, so that it becomes possible to form a picture of the actual stream of mental activity and attention.

The patient may be inaccessible as in coma, stupor, delirium, excitement, or because of self-absorption, or indifference. In these conditions, however, one may make a good description of the attitude and general reactions and note the fragmentary replies. *Or,* the responses may show the other extreme—that of profusion of activity or speech. In such cases one may obtain samples which may be eminently characteristic.

In order to simplify the recording data on stream of mental activity you may use the accompanying outline:

1. *Verbal productivity*

   Profuse, normal, diminished.

2. *Spontaneity of stream of thought*

   Spontaneous flow, halting and hesitant, very constricted flow.

3. *Distractibility*

   Irrelevant, incoherent, flighty.

   Test for distractibility: show an object, make a sound, or speak certain words and get patient's association to them. Distractible patients may begin with acceptable association but wander off very soon.

4. *Language deviations of patient*

   Sound associations, neologisms (self-invented words or phrases), echolalia, stereotypy.

5. *Reaction time in responding*

   Time between end of a short question and beginning of response by patient. Record in seconds, or with stopwatch in fifths of a second.

IV. Emotional Reactions

Since abnormalities of the emotions are among the most striking manifestations of mental disorder, a careful analysis of these reactions is extremely important. The emotional state will, of course, have to be considered especially in relation to the mental trend and the general activity of the patient. In general the objective and subjective aspects of the emotional reactions should be noted: what is seen (the facial expression, the attitudes and postures) and what the patient says about his feelings.

The examiner should note whether the patient is quiescent, composed, complacent, or without any special emotional display.

Or irritable, angry, happy, elated, exalted.

Or boastful, egotistical, self-satisfied.

Or suspicious, distant, disdainful.

Or depressed, sad, hopeless, anxious, fearful, perplexed.

Or indifferent, apathetic, dull.

Often there is striking variability in mood with or without apparent external causes.

Of special importance is the relation between emotional expression and thought content. One should note carefully any inappropriate emotional reactions or discrepancies between the patient's ideas and the accompanying mood. Such a dissociation may be indicated by an indifferent or smiling reaction in the face of ideas which would normally call forth a depressive, anxious, or distressed response.

Even when the patient is unresponsive one may make important observations regarding the emotions by noting the behavior of pulse and respiration, or the appearance of flushing, perspiration, or tears, or changes in facial expression.

If the feelings are not spontaneously described by the patient, *appropriate* questions may be asked, as:

How do you feel
Are you happy
Are you indifferent   Satisfied
Are you sad   Troubled over something
Are you afraid
Are you worried

V. Mental Trend: Content of Thought

The examiner may have already learned from the preceding parts of the examination something of the patient's general mental trend.

The patient may be willing and able to give a good account of the beginning and subsequent course of the mental disorder. He should, therefore, have an opportunity to *tell his story in full.* The patient should be encouraged to talk freely and to recount in detail the steps in the development of his difficulties. The aim should be to get a full report of the patient's trend of ideas or thought content.

In hospital or committed cases the patient's account of just what led to admission should be obtained and particular inquiry made regarding any anti-social acts or tendencies.

If, as is often the case, the patient is reluctant to talk or is inclined to conceal his ideas, the examiner should proceed with appropriate questions.

If there are any indications of a *persecutory trend* ask concerning:

Sensitiveness of being watched.

Suspicion of being talked about.

Inclination to see a meaning in things that would not ordinarily be seen.

Unpleasant family relations, jealousy, suspicions of sexual nature.

Suspicions of being wronged, annoyed, robbed, poisoned.

Feelings of bodily influence by machines or electricity, or mind-reading, hypnotism, etc. How is it done and why By whom.

Interference with thinking by outside influences.

Is there a combined plan in all this.

What makes the patient think so.

Hypochondriacal ideas or somatic delusions may be brought out by appropriate questions as to health and strength, functions of the internal organs, bowel action, sexual power, condition of the blood, etc.

Ideas of unreality may be expressed in that the outside world has changed, that everything looks different, or that the individual has changed, that the body is unnatural, feelings gone, life has ceased, he is no longer a human being, etc.

Nihilistic ideas may be expressed by statements that everything is lost or destroyed, nothing exists, there is no life, no matter, no universe, etc.

Other depressive trends will often be indicated in the paragraph on Emotional Reactions. Inquiry should be made, however, regarding tendency to self-criticism and depreciation, ideas of sinfulness and self-condemnation, of the soul being lost, etc.

Grandiose ideas are more apt to be freely expressed in exalted emotional states. A few questions may be asked concerning ideas of strength, power, wealth, high birth, etc.

Hallucinatory experiences may be elicited by the following questions:

Has anything strange happened.

Have you imaginations.

Do you have peculiar thoughts.

Do you hear things.

Have you heard any talking from the neighbors, or people on the street.

Do you see things.

One may find the patient listening and mumbling or gesticulating: or he may suddenly turn, guard himself, become sullen, or talk. The record must, however, limit itself carefully to what evidence can actually be gained. The current term "talking to imaginary persons" is very frequently not referable at all to hallucinations, especially in manic states. Visions, fear of poison, hallucinations of smell and of physical influence call forth similarly characteristic reactions.

Any such experience of sense deceptions, influence, etc., are to be subjected to a careful inquiry along the following lines:

In the case of hallucinations of hearing:

Do you hear voices or noises.

Where and when   On what occasion   In which ear (may be unilateral).

Plainly   Men or women   Do you recognize the voices.

Real voices, whispers, sounds or thoughts.

What do the voices say in conversation to or about you.

Are they pleasant or unpleasant.

Do you respond Do they surprise or scare you.

Can you stop the talk or can others By speaking or listening to other things What brings on the talk Is it worse at times.

In the case of *visual hallucinations,* inquire what is seen, whether they occur in daylight or dark, with the eyes open or shut.

Do the hallucinated objects move or speak Give details What attitude do they seem to have toward the patient.

Can hallucinations be provoked (pressure on the eye, or gazing at a blank sheet of paper or wall).

Are there hallucinations of *smell, taste or touch* If these are indicated elicit full details from patient regarding the source, time of occurrence and his explanation.

Are there *illusions* or *misinterpretations.*

Has the patient insight into the hallucinations at the time or later.

In the case of other *"peculiar thoughts"* (obsessions, compulsions, phobias) or *feelings* (anxieties, fears) or *actions* (compulsive acts) inquire along the following lines:

Do you have thoughts that bother you.

How do they come to you.

What are they about.

Do uncomfortable feelings come to you Give the circumstances.

Do you feel compelled to do certain things against your will Give the circumstances.

In order to determine the dynamic factors underlying the patient's problems it is usually necessary to have repeated interviews and finally to make a careful summary of the entire material. This further study must often extend over a considerable period and the results will naturally have to be recorded in notes made subsequent to the mental status.

VI. Sensorium, Mental Grasp and Capacity

In all cases inquiry in this field is essential in order to establish an estimate of the intellectual capacities and resources of the individual. Neglect in this direction is the most common defect of many records of cases in which an error of diagnosis must subsequently be admitted. Especially the records of non-recognized organic conditions, such as general paresis, show very often that a thorough search for gaps of memory and for discrepancies in the giving of chronological data has not been made. Moreover, where the patient has been found unable to give a spontaneous account, the questions here proposed should bring out important and valuable responses on which to base comparisons with previous capacities.

The following questions indicate the lines along which inquiries should be made. The questions should be regarded as leads in the examination; they should be supplemented by other questions to bring out full details. In cases where some defect or abnormality is observed in the examination, the question and answer form of recording results is preferable. In other cases the patient's responses may be given in the form of indirect discourse.

a. Orientation as to Time, Place and Person:

1. Place

   What place is this What is it for Where is it located.

   What city Tell me the way to your room, ward.

2. Person

   Who am I and what am I doing here Does patient identify nurses and patients as such.

3. Time

   What is the date: Year, month, day of month, day of week.

   What time of day is it How long have you been here—how long sick How long ago was New Year's, Fourth of July.

b. Data of Personal Identification, Remote Memory:

The following questions are aimed primarily to test the grasp of the more remote experiences and the ability to correlate dates and give facts in chronological order. Some physicians prefer to go further and use these questions, supplemented by others, as a basis for an account by the patient of his family and personal life history. There is no objection to proceeding in this manner if it is understood that a regular anamnesis from relatives or friends is to be obtained and recorded in the usual way as soon as possible.

If the patient is capable of giving reliable information the physician may at this point turn to the statistical data sheet, in hospitals or clinics where these are used, and fill in as much of the information called for as is deemed desirable. It is especially important to do this in the case of patients who have no visitors or friends, as the information called for is needed for administrative purposes, statistics and death certificates.

Where were you born.

Date of birth.

How old does that make you.

Where and how long did you go to school Highest grade completed.

When did you begin work Name and address of first and subsequent employers.

What was your mother's name before she was married.

If the patient is foreign-born, ask:

When did you come to the United States.

With whom On what ship and line.

How old were you then.

Naturalized citizen of the U. S. If so, give date and particulars.

How long in New York State (or in the state and city of last residence).

Date of marriage How old were you then.

Names and birthdays of children.

Where were you last employed Name and address of employer.

Previous illnesses, accidents, injuries and hospital residences Give the dates.

Family data: names and birthplaces of parents; living or dead.

Number of children (brothers and sisters of patient).

c. Memory of the Recent Past:

Where do you live Street and number With whom.

How long have you lived there.

When did you leave home.

Where did you go, and with whom.

How did you come here How did you travel here.

Who came with you.

What was done for you on admission.

How long here.

Where were you yesterday A week ago.

How many meals have you had today.

What is my name When did you see me for the first time What are the newspaper headlines saying these days.

For clinic or other patients who have not been hospitalized the questions to test the memory of recent past should be modified to suit the particular situation.

d. Retention and Immediate Recall

a. Retention of auditory material

To test auditory retention, say to patient: I am going to give you the name of a person and his address. Listen carefully and afterwards I am going to ask you for them. Test after 5 minutes, one hour, and one day, if possible.

b. Retention of visual material

Point to an object possessing color (necktie, blotter, etc.) and to time on watch and say: I want you to remember this article and its color and the time when I showed it to you. Test similarly after 5 minutes, one hour, and one day, if possible.

c. Auditory Memory Span—Digits Forward

Say to patient: I am going to say some numbers. Listen carefully and when I am through, say them right after me.

4-6-9-2	7-3-8-4-6-9-2
5-3-8-1-7	8-2-9-6-4-7-1-5
2-9-6-4-8-3	3-5-1-7-4-6-9-2-8

Record the result of the tests and show how far the patient can go without mistakes. If there is any retention disorder additional tests should be carried out as follows:

Execution of series of orders: Three-paper test as follows:

Use three pieces of paper of different sizes and give instructions for disposal of each, e. g., "Place the largest piece on the desk, put the middle-size piece in your pocket and give me the smallest piece." Record exactly what the patient does.

Word pairs. In carrying out this test, the examiner first describes to the patient the nature of the test—that he, the patient, is to be asked to remember words that belong together; that the examiner will read aloud several pairs of such words, that the patient is to repeat each pair as given, to fix them in his mind, that then the examiner is to give the first word of each pair and that the patient is to respond with the second word of each pair. When certain that the patient understands what is to be done, carry out the test with the following words and record verbatim the patient's replies:

Head	—	hair	Window	—	door
Room	—	hall	Book	—	pencil
Chair	—	table	Lake	—	river
Grass	—	tree	Apple	—	pear
White	—	red	Pipe	—	tobacco

e. Counting and Calculation:

Ask the patient to carry out the following tests:

To count from 1 to 20 as rapidly as possible.

To count backwards, from 20 to 1.

To count coins.

To do simple calculations:

4 times 9	5 and 4	12 divided by 6
6 times 16	14 and 9	63 divided by 7

To subtract 7 from 100 and keep subtracting 7 until 2 is reached. Record exactly the responses.

To compute 1½ year's interest on $200 at 4 per cent.

To solve: If 5 times x equals 20, how much is x.

In all the tests give the *time required* for answers in secouds or minutes. Also describe the effort made by the patient to cooperate, and if there are delays, slowness or errors, how does the patient explain them.

f. Reading:

The patient is told that he is to be asked to read a short story aloud and then to tell what it is about. The following story is used: [See page 88 for patient's use.]

The Cowboy Story

A cowboy—from Arizona—went—to San Francisco—with his dog—which he left—at a friend's—while he purchased—a new suit of clothes. Dressed—in the new suit—he went back—to the dog—whistled to him—called him by name—and patted him. But the dog—would have nothing to do with him—in his new hat—and coat—but gave a mournful howl. Coaxing—had no effect—so the cowboy—went away—and donned—his old garments—whereupon the dog—immediately showed—his wild joy—on seeing his master—as he thought he ought to be.

The examiner can check each of the subdivisions of the story as the patient retells it and the number of memories can give some indication of the degree of retention. There are 32 subdivisions and a patient who remembers at least 20 correctly or approximately correctly may be regarded as giving an average performance. The examiner may record for each printed phrase the actual phrase given by the patient.

Character of reading: facile, labored, words mispronounced, left out.

Does the patient understand the story.

In repeating does he give any irrelevant details.

If there is any indication of deficiency in pronunciation the following test may be used as a check. Ask the patient to say the following words:

1. leave
2. frivolity
3. anticipation
4. imperturbable
5. Methodist Episcopal
6. statistical

Patients who mispronounce more than half of these words should be referred to the psychologist for further examination.

g. Writing:

Ask the patient to write you a note (how he is feeling, what kind of a day it is, how he liked the examination, etc.). Use unlined paper and have him write it as freely and spontaneously as he can (do not designate margins or indicate what part of paper to use).

Note whether his writing is free, slow or constrained, and whether it shows tremor or elisions and transpositions of letters or syllables. Is the writing unduly large or unduly small, is it unusual in any other respect (slanting backwards, heavyhanded or light). Run tips of fingers over back of paper to see whether writing pressure has left ridges.

If possible obtain handwriting specimens written before illness and as far back in the development of the patient as possible. A comparison of the handwriting specimens sometimes gives clues as to time of onset and type of difficulty.

h. School and General Knowledge:

It is desirable to investigate the ability to reproduce what was learned at school and also to test the range of the patient's general information and grasp of current events. The tests, of course, should be made with due regard to nationality, educational level, and general experiences of the individual. Tests already made under Counting and Calculation, Reading and Writing will have given a good deal of information as to school knowledge and mental level.

Questions such as the following may be given as further aids in determining the patient's school and general knowledge:

In giving these questions begin with the middle group of questions—5, 6, 7, 8—and if the patient passes these successfully, he may be regarded as possessing as much general information as the average person. If he fails on these questions, go back to the first set of questions—1, 2, 3, 4. This arrangement will save time and permit the examiner to cover more ground. If the examiner wishes to determine how high the level of information of the patient reaches, he may, after the subject has answered the middle four questions, go on to the highest level—questions 9, 10, 11, 12.

These questions should be asked in a conversational tone, and the manner in which the patient answers may reveal not only whether or not he possesses the required information, but also other aspects of his personality.*

1. Name some vegetables.
2. What is the largest river in the United States?
3. Why did the Pilgrims come to this country?
4. For how many years is the President of the United States elected?

*Selected from Scaled Information Test (Bronner, Healy, Lowe, Shimberg) by Grace H. Kent. J. Psychol., 1942, *13*, p. 158.

5. What three things do most plants need in order to live?

6. Name some insects.

7. What is a civil war?

8. How is it that newspapers can be sold for less than the cost of printing?

9. What is the freezing point of water?

10. What is the usual economic result of the overproduction of any commodity?

11. What is the function of respiration?

12. What is a referendum in government?

i. Intelligence Rating:

The intellectual level of the patient may be judged to a considerable extent by the results of the preceding parts of the examination. If there is reason to believe that the individual is subnormal in intelligence, a psychometric determination is indicated. This, of course, cannot be done satisfactorily unless the patient is accessible and cooperative. Care should be taken in judging the results of psychometric tests. In some psychotic states, because of the abnormal emotional reactions, lack of effort, inattention, inhibition, negativism, delusional ideas, etc., a mental age rating may be misleading or worthless as an estimate of the patient's true intellectual capacity.

In order to obtain a rough estimate of whether the patient is at least of normal intelligence, the Kent EGY test* is to be used as given below:

Procedure: Ask the questions in a conversational manner with reasonable latitude in phraseology. Score each response as you go along in accordance with the directions given after each item. Add up the credits for all the items and record them as the total score. If this score is less than 22, you may infer that the patient is possibly subnormal in

*Kent, Grace H. Emergency Battery of One-Minute Tests. J. Psychol., 1942, *13*, p. 157.

Oral Test for Emergency Use in Clinics. Mental Measurements Monographs. 1932. No. 9. The Williams and Wilkins Co.

intelligence and should be given a complete psychometric test to establish his mental level. If the score is 25 or over, the patient is presumably within normal limits with respect to intelligence and should not require any further psychometric examination unless there is a definite need to know his exact mental level.

The three additional items are to be used as alternates for any of the first 10 items that the examiner considers unsuitable.

If the patient obtains a score of between 22-25 on the Kent EGY test, the examiner should refer him to the psychologist for a complete psychometric examination. It is well to bear in mind that the psychometric examination may yield, in addition to an accurate estimate of intelligence, some indications of specific personality deviations in the patient. The information gleaned from the method of attack used on the test by the patient, from the performance pattern that he exhibits, and from the scatter of his successes and failures often indicates whether the patient shows psychotic or neurotic trends and whether there is any evidence of organic involvement. For this reason, a general test of intelligence is sometimes desirable even when the patient is apparently not subnormal mentally.

1. What are houses made of? (Any materials you can think of) 1-4

   One point for each item, up to four.

2. What is sand used for? .... 1, 2, or 4

   Four points for manufacture of glass. Two points for mixing with concrete, road building, or other constructive use. One point for play or scrubbing. Credits not cumulative.

3. If the flag floats to the south, from what direction is the wind? 3

   Three points for north, no partial credits.

   It is permissible to say: 'Which way is the wind coming from?'

4. Tell me the names of some fishes 1-4

One point each, up to four. If the subject stops with one, encourage him to go on.

5. At what time of day is your shadow shortest?.. 3

Noon, three points. If correct response is suspected of being a guess, inquire why.

6. Give the names of some large cities 1-4

One point for each, up to four. When any state is named as a city, no credit, i. e. New York unless specified as New York City. No credit for home town except when it is an outstanding city.

7. Why does the moon look larger than the stars?.. 2, 3, 4

Make it clear that the question refers to any particular star, and give assurance that the moon is actually smaller than any star. Encourage the subject to guess. Two points for 'Moon is lower down.' Three points for nearer or closer. Four points for generalized statement that nearer objects look larger than more distant objects.

8. What metal is attracted by a magnet? ....2 or 4

Four points for iron, two for steel.

9. If your shadow points to the northeast, where is the sun? 4

Four points for southwest, no partial credits.

10. How many stripes in the flag?................ 2

Thirteen, two points. A subject who responds 48 may be permitted to correct his mistake. Explain, if necessary, that the white stripes are included as well as the red ones.

What does ice become when it melts?.......... 1

Water, one point.

How many minutes in an hour? 1

Sixty, one point.

Why is it colder at night than in the daytime?.. 1-3

Two points for 'sun goes down,' or any recognition of direct rays of sun as source of heat. Additional point for rotation of earth. Question may be reversed: 'What makes it warmer in the daytime than at night?' Only one point for answer to reversed question.

j. Other Special Mental Functions

The psychological and psychiatric examination outlined here is calculated to give the examiner sufficient data to establish the major findings about most cases. Sometimes, however, in the course of the mental examination, certain trends appear which may require further investigation. Thus, the presence of mental deterioration may be suspected, or some impairment may be noted in ability to make generalizations, ability to maintain a given trend of thought, or exercise good judgment. In order to establish the clinical impression on a somewhat more certain basis, the following tests are provided. Whenever these tests corroborate the examiner's impression about a given trend or trait in the patient, he should call for a more detailed examination by the psychologist.

1. Deteriorative Process

Observations of attitude and general behavior (I—p. 61) and emotional reactions (IV—p. 66) will yield considerable evidence for or against the deteriorative process. Parts of the mental examination dealing with the sensorium, mental grasp and capacity (VI—p. 71) can yield some objective evidence in this direction.

(a) Evidence from Schooling

If the general performance on these interview questions and tests is lower than what would be expected from the school history, deterioration may be suspected. The age at leaving school together with the highest grade reached at that time can serve as an index of brightness. This age-grade index should show no greater disparity than 2 or 2½ years for the normal person. Thus a child leaving the 8th grade at 15-16 years of age may still be regarded as average, but one who leaves that grade at 16½ or later (without any extenuating circumstances provided by medical or environmental factors) may be suspected of being dull, and his performance at the time of admission to the hospital judged accordingly. The number of times he was skipped or left back in the grades should offer corroborating evidence for this judgment.

(b) Evidence from Mental Efficiency

It has been demonstrated that the vocabulary of a patient deteriorates less rapidly than any of the other mental functions. The vocabulary level may be regarded within certain limits as an estimate of his basic intelligence while the level exhibited on the other tests may be taken as an index of how well he uses his mental endowment—or mental efficiency. Accordingly some estimate of degree of deterioration can be obtained by comparing the results on the vocabulary test (p. 86) with the results on the other tests such as digits forward (p. 74), subtraction of 7's from 100 (p. 75), mental age on the Kent EGY (p. 79) and the general estimate of behavior shown by the patient. In all such cases the patient should be referred to the psychologist for more careful measures of deterioration by such tests as the Shipley Hartford Scale, Babcock Deterioration Test, B R L, Vigotsky, etc.

2. Abstraction Ability

The ability to abstract becomes impaired or at least deviates from the normal in schizophrenic patients and in some types of organic cases. If such impairment is suspected, the similarities test may be given.* This test gives an indication of the level of abstraction that characterizes the subject. Thus, a patient who says an apple and an orange are alike because they both have skins is on a lower level of maturity in thinking than one who says they are both fruit.

The pair tomato-beet is used as a sample because of the variety of possible responses. The folowing similarities should be mentioned by the examiner if the patient fails to mention them: they are both plants, garden vegetables, edible, red in color, and the tomato is usually larger than the beet. After enumerating the trifling similarities the patient's attention should be called to the most important similarity—they are both plants. The patient is then requested to name the most important similarity for each word pair. The pairs have been arranged in order of difficulty in three colums. Start with the middle column and if the patient suceeds with all six pairs in the middle column, the test may be ended since the subject is at least average. If he fails in some of the middle column, go back to the first column and see how many of these he succeeds in. The difficult list may be used for very successful patients.

bird..... butterfly	church. theatre	mountain plateau
gate..... door	nest.... kennel	map..... directory
river.... brook	cigar... cigarette	shadow.. reflection
bread.... cake	calf.... colt	whale... shark
coachman chauffeur	water.. wine	dregs... scum
skating.. dancing	hammer hatchet	star..... planet

*Kent, Grace H. Emergency Battery of One-Minute Tests. J. Psychol. 1942, *13*, p. 152.

The experienced examiner can select the word-pairs he considers most suitable for the case before him and ignore the above directions. But the beginning examiner should follow the above rules until he gets completely familiar with the test.

Another test of abstraction is the Absurdity Test.* This test has been found to differentiate lower from higher levels of abstraction and some schizophrenics find it especially difficult to do well on it. There are no norms available for this test yet, and the patient's performance must be evaluated qualitatively.

Say to the patient: What is foolish, absurd, (does not make good sense) about this:

1. They put the cake of ice on the stove to keep it from melting.
2. It was late winter, and the leaves were brilliant with many colors.
3. A few more turns of the hammer, and the bolt was down to the head.
4. The angry hen chased the duck to the other side of the river.
5. The ship was loaded with empty beer casks and went down at once.
6. As he crossed the finish line ahead of his rivals, he saw them still running in front of him.
7. Silver must be more valuable than lead, because gold is more valuable than either of them.
8. As he looked at the engine a mile away, he heard the whistle blow, and then he saw the cloud of steam which came out of the whistle.
9. A foot must be longer than an inch, because three feet make a yard.
10. It was five o'clock in the afternoon; and, by hurrying, he thought he could get home by two the same day.

*Wells, F. L., and Ruesch, J. Mental Examiner's Handbook, p. 13. Psychological Corporation. New York. 1942.

3. Ability to Maintain Set or Associative Trend

A test which indicates to what extent the patient is able to control his associative processes and maintain a given set or trend of thought is the Opposites Test.* Flighty patients do not do well on this test while extremely pedantic or depressed patients may find difficulty in giving opposites. Say to the patient: What is the opposite of good? If the subject does not respond promptly it may be necessary to explain the meaning of opposite: Bad is the opposite of good because it is as different as possible. Continue with cold, what is as different as possible from cold? If it isn't cold, what might it be? If this explanation does not suffice, it may be considered a waste of time to continue any further with the test.

Begin with the middle column as before, and proceed to the first column if the patient's performance is poor on the middle column.

heavy	above	deep
winter	strong	expel
tight	remember	affirm
near	war	prove
smooth	broad	frequently
lost	future	dangerous
dead	wild	urban
first	best	transparent
success	false	arrive
stale	public	simple

Proceed to third column if the patient is very successful with the middle column.

If the patient succeeds with the middle column, he is not deficient in this ability.

4. Thinking Process

If there is an indication of a schizophrenic process its effect may sometimes become most apparent in the vocabulary test. The presence of neologisms are, of

*Kent, Grace H. op. cit. p. 148.

course, suggestive of a schizophrenic process, but even in patients who do not show this type of aberration more subtle aberrations may be noted. Wechsler has collected some examples of definitions given by schizophrenics, e. g., *Lecture*—"a method of discipline or training given many groups of assembled people," or "to profess in school." *Rule*—"to continue as sole master." *Envelope*—"an article of communication used to convey a message of importance," or "a receptacle for papers."

Directions for beginning the test:* Now I am going to read you a list of words and I want you to tell me what they mean. What does .... mean?

1. orange
2. puddle
3. eyelash
4. muzzle
5. Mars
6. brunette
7. regard
8. tolerate
9. bewail
10. flaunt
11. frustrate
12. harpy
13. depredation
14. achromatic
15. sudorific

When the patient refuses two or three words in succession after having responded to the previous words there is no need to go on further. The chief value of this type of test is to permit any aberrations in the thought process to make themselves apparent. But if some estimate of mental ability is desired, it may be noted that 5, 6 and 7 words correct correspond roughly to mental ages of 12, 13 and 14 respectively.

k. Insight and Judgment

Does the patient realize that he has suffered a physical or mental change or breakdown and that he needs treatment? Does he acknowledge that he has strange imaginations or ideas? Does he realize that the difficulty is within himself or does he ascribe it to external sources?

*Thorndike, R. L. Two Screening Tests of Verbal Intelligence. J. Applied Psychol. 1942, *26*, 128-135. List 3, p. 134.

Is the patient aware of defects of memory or other failure of capacity which may be present?

Does the patient show good or poor judgment in his general activities? Is his judgment better on impersonal than personal matters?

What are the plans for the future?

If the examiner suspects an impairment of judgment he can give the following questions which frequently serve to give an indication of judgment impairment such as is found in psychopathic personalities. It is in reality a test of so-called common sense.*

1. What is the thing to do if you find an envelope in the street, that is sealed, stamped and addressed?
2. Why should we keep away from bad company?
3. Why are shoes made of leather?
4. Why does land in the city cost more than land in the country?
5. Why does the state require people to get a license in order to get married?

The above questions are taken from the Bellevue-Wechsler Test which may be used subsequently by the psychologist for determining the intellectual level of the patient. In order not to spoil the value of the test for the patient, the examiner should refrain from giving away the correct answers to the above questions.

VII. Summary of Mental Examination

A summary of the main findings established during the mental examination should be made.

The tests suggested should give several overall impressions of the subject's intellectual capacities, their organization, and how they have been modified by the mental disorder.

1. Evenness of Performance. The examiner should be able to decide on the basis of the performance whether the

*Wechsler, D. Measurement of Adult Intelligence. Second edition. The Williams and Wilkins Co. 1941, p. 168.

patient is on an even mental keel, or whether his performance is spotty. If the latter, there should be some indication of whether the unevenness is a permanent feature of the patient or whether it is only due to a temporary disturbance. In cases of doubt, the patient should be referred to the psychologist for further examination.

2. Deteriorative Trend. Methods for determining the possible presence of deterioration have been indicated previously.

3. Self Evaluation. The degree to which the subject correctly estimates his own abilities and worth can only be determined by an overall evaluation of his entire performance and by proper questioning about how he regards his performance.

Recorded observations made of the patient subsequent to the initial examination as outlined above should be made to show the course of the patient's disorder, whether improved, stationary or worse. Facts rather than conclusions should be recorded, with the results of retests in the various divisions of the examination outlined to demonstrate concretely the patient's condition. The frequency of these noted observations may be determined by hospital regulations, by the frequency of clinic visits, or by the physician's interest and time available. Under any circumstances the primary purpose is to make a clear acceptable record of observations which will mean something to other physicians and react with benefit to the patient.

The Cowboy Story

A cowboy from Arizona went to San Francisco with his dog which he left at a friend's while he purchased a new suit of clothes. Dressed in the new suit he went back to the dog, whistled to him, called him by name and patted him. But the dog would have nothing to do with him in his new hat and coat, but gave a mournful howl. Coaxing had no effect, so the cowboy went away and donned his old garments, whereupon the dog immediately showed his wild joy on seeing his master as he thought he ought to be.

VI

FURTHER SPECIAL MENTAL EXAMINATION

The facts obtained from the Mental Examination will, in many instances, give the main characteristics of the clinical syndrome with which one is dealing in the individual patient; they will often enable one to arrive at a formulation of the principal problem. In many instances, however, particularly in the constitutional or psychogenic disorders, one can only arrive at an understanding of the underlying forces which have brought about the symptomatology by a further detailed, and sometimes very extensive investigation of the patient's conscious and unconscious life.

Some patients, particularly those in overproductive excitement, delirium or hallucinatory states, at which time the usual inhibitions are to a large extent removed and free association holds sway, may freely express previously unconscious ideas, conflicts and tendencies. From these expressions one gains some conception of the underlying problems. With such patients, therefore, one should make a record, preferably stenographic, of the productions in order to get samples of the topics or dominant trends which appear during these phases. Then, when the patient is more accessible or convalescent, these productions should be reviewed with him to get further associations and the meaning of the ideas or expressions to the patient. In this way mechanisms may be understood not only by the physician but by the patient. One may expect, however, that frequently these same patients, when they are convalescent and more accessible in one sense, in that they can respond to examination more logically and rationally, may in another sense be less accessible; that is, with the regaining of conscious control, the previously expressed ideas or trends may have been forgotten or repressed. They may be unrecognized by the patient and he is unable to explain them or tends not to associate other ideas freely with them.

In such events, as well as with other patients who may be cooperative and intelligent and in whom the thinking is not disordered by brain disease, an understanding of the underlying forces leading to the breakdown demands a detailed life study of the patient, with consideration of the facts given by others as well as those obtained from him. Such an investigation includes an account from the patient of his earliest emotional experiences and his reactions to them; an account of infantile interests and attachments; his attitude toward his family, other persons, and the world in general; his frustrations and his reaction to them; and other facts that may be elicited. Many of the ideas and feelings may be disclosed by the patient for the first time; they may be things about which he has worried to the point of breakdown. Much, therefore, may be obtained from the patient's conscious mental life to explain his symptoms and lead to an understanding of them.

Often, however, and particularly in psychoneurotic reactions, the symptoms are not understandable to the physician or the patient by the usual processes of rational, logical conscious thinking. The physician knows then that they are the products of the unconscious mind, and for an understanding of them the unconscious must be brought to consciousness.

This outline is not intended as a guide to psycholanalysis, by which term is meant the analytic technique described by Freud. But some of the principles of investigation of the unconscious may be applied to advantage in psychiatric examinations.

Free association: As indicated above, in certain disturbed, delirious or hallucinatory states, the normal inhibition exerted on the unconscious by the conscious is removed, and the patient is more or less controlled by the unconscious which speaks freely in an illogical, "irrational" way, in the "strange" productions or hallucinations or delirious utterances. In the patient who is more rational, that is, who is controlled more by his conscious thinking, an approach to this uninhibited free state may be attained by having him, in a quiet setting free from all distraction, along with the physician let his mind drift as it will, giving expression freely and with complete mental and physical relaxation to any ideas that come to his mind, without regard to logic, coherence or rationality. This is the method of free association. In such a relaxed uninhibited state, ideas previously forcibly kept out of the mind (repressed) tend to come to the surface, often to the surprise of the patient. Associations to the "strange" ideas are continued so that their connections and meanings become clear to the patient. Thus by himself, he arrives at an explanation to himself and to the examiner of the symptoms that may have had no meaning before.

The physician is not to make the explanation of what certain ideas mean when asked to do so by the patient but he may suggest several possibilities for the patient to work out himself. As previously indicated in the Mental Examination the physician is not to force his interpretation of the symptoms on the patient.

Some patients will appear to be associating freely by talking freely and at length. Such associations, however, may be superficial, sometimes association merely by the sound of words, without depth or thinking, or the productions may be a repetition of the symptomatology in the minutest details. Such a reaction may be a "talking away from the subject"—a method of protecting or covering up the unconscious, so that one understands very little after a long time. In such cases and in other cases where the patient seems to have nothing to say or is "empty" of thought, the examiner may ask the patient to associate to some particular idea or action that the previous examination or anamnesis has brought out. The examiner, however, should avoid suggesting his own ideas to the patient or indicating whether he approves or disapproves of the patient's thoughts about anything.

An added method of free association is afforded by the use of dream material which the patient remembers and recounts to the examiner. Here again the patient does the interpreting by indicating what associations are brought to his mind by the dream material. The physician is not to tell the patient what the dream means; he may have some conceptions but these are irrelevant—the meaning and interpretation have to come from within the patient.

By these two methods of free association—the association to ideas occurring in the waking state and the associations to material in dreams—the unconscious may be brought to consciousness. Unconscious tendencies or ideas which have acted as forces in bringing about symptomatology in actions, feeling or thinking may be brought to light and understood, and so the symptomatology may be understood. The psychiatric examination and understanding of many psychiatric reactions cannot be complete without some such method and it is to be advocated for suitable, cooperative, intelligent, thinking patients who have insight and the desire to get well.

EXAMINATION OF UNCOOPERATIVE PATIENTS

(Synopsis)

I. General Reaction and Posture

II. Facial Movements and Expression

III. Eyes and Pupils

IV. Reaction to What Is Said or Done

V. Muscular Reactions

VI. Emotional Responsiveness

VII. Speech

VIII. Writing

IX. Summary

VII

EXAMINATION OF UNCOOPERATIVE PATIENTS

Even though a patient is not cooperative certain observations of value may be made. These may be of importance in the study of various types of cases and give data for the understanding of different clinical reactions. The time to study negativistic reactions is during the period of negativism; the time to study a stupor is during the stuporous phase. To wait for the clinical picture to change or for the patient to become more accessible is often to miss an opportunity and leave a gap in the clinical observation. It is necessary in the examination of such cases to adopt some plan other than that used in taking the usual mental status. The following guide was devised to cover the most important points in the examination of uncooperative patients.

I. GENERAL REACTION AND POSTURE:

Spontaneous acts: any occasional show of playfulness, mischievousness or assaultiveness. Defense movements when interfered with or when pricked with pin. Does the patient eat voluntarily or must he be fed. Describe in detail how he acts while eating or being fed. Does the patient dress and undress himself or does he require assistance. Is he neat or untidy. Do his actions show only initial retardation or consistent slowness throughout.

Behavior toward physicians and nurses: resistive, evasive, irritable, apathetic, compliant.

Voluntary postures: comfortable, natural, constrained or awkward.

What does the patient do if placed in awkward or uncomfortable positions.

Is the behavior constant or variable from time to time.

Do any special occurrences influence patient's behavior.

II. FACIAL MOVEMENTS AND EXPRESSION:

(See Synopsis)

Is the expression alert, attentive, smiling, placid, mask-like, stolid, sulky, scowling, perplexed, distressed, tearful.

Is the facial expression constant or variable; if the latter, on what occasions; is grimacing present.

III. EYES AND PUPILS:

Are the eyes open or closed; if closed does he resist having lid raised.

Movement of eyes: Does he give attention and follow the examiner or moving objects; or show only fixed gazing, furtive glances or evasion.

Is there rolling of eyeballs upward.

Size and reaction of pupils.

Is there blinking, flickering or tremor of lids.

What is the reaction to sudden approach or threat to stick pin in eye.

What is the sensory reaction of pupils (dilatation from painful stimuli or from irritation of the skin of the neck).

Is there corneal irritability (with or without appearance of tears).

IV. REACTIONS TO WHAT IS SAID OR DONE:

What is the response to commands: show tongue, move limbs, grasp with hand (climbing, clutching, etc.).

Are motions slow or sudden or natural.

What is the reaction to pin pricks.

Is there automatic obedience: Tell the patient to protrude the tongue to have a pin stuck into it.

Is there echopraxia (imitation of actions of others).

Is there echolalia (imitation of speech of others).

V. MUSCULAR REACTIONS:

Test for rigidity: Are the muscles relaxed or tense when limbs or body is moved; is there waxy flexibility; is there negativism (shown by movements in opposite direction or springy or cog-wheel resistance); test the reflexes.

Test flexibility of neck muscles by movements forward and backward and from side to side. Test also the flexibility of the muscles of the jaw, shoulders, elbows, fingers and the lower extremities.

Does distraction or command influence the reactions.

Is the mouth usually open or closed. Is there resistance to opening or closing the mouth. Is there protrusion of lips (*schnauzkrampf*).

Is there holding of saliva or drooling.

Is there retention of urine and feces or soiling and wetting. Does he indicate when he wants to go to the toilet.

VI. EMOTIONAL RESPONSIVENESS:

Is feeling shown when members of family are spoken of or when certain personal facts are mentioned, or when visitors come. Note whether or not there is acceleration of pulse or respiration or flushing, perspiration, tears at such times.

Do jokes, references to family, or sad news elicit any change in facial expression or other response.

What is the effect of unexpected stimuli (clapping of hands, flash of electric light).

VII. SPEECH:

Is the patient consistently mute or are there periods when he speaks. Is speech spontaneous.

Note exact utterances with accompanying emotional reaction.

Is there any apparent effort to talk, shown by lip movement, whispers or nodding or shaking of the head.

VIII. WRITING:

Offer the patient paper and pencil and ask him to write anything he wishes. If there is no response dictate a sentence to him. (Irresponsive or partially stuporous patients will often write when they fail to talk).

IX. SUMMARY:

A summary of the main findings of this examination should be made.

VIII

PSYCHIATRIC EXAMINATION OF CHILDREN

(Synopsis)

INTRODUCTION

In the psychiatric examination of children many of the points of inquiry are the same as those already outlined for the study of adults. However, because of the differences in the problems and in the approaches to the parents and child, it has been considered advisable to include in this volume a special guide for the examination of children. By children is meant those individuals not over 12 years of age. Ordinarily, parents possess more vivid details of the early lives of their children when the children are young. Moreover, the child's life and experiences are so intimately a part of the family life that information from the parents or guardians is indispensable. Also, the younger the child the less one may learn directly from him and the more necessary is an informant. The study of psychiatric problems in children is generally not concerned with distinct clinical syndromes but with the total personality.

It is desirable to encourage the informant, who is usually the parent, to discuss the problem spontaneously and without regard to any order indicated in the outline. It is only when the spontaneity of the informant begins to wane that direct and specific interrogation becomes advisable.

Anamnesis

I. *The Problem*—The problem, that is, the reason why the child is being examined, should be stated at the outset in concise terms. If the child is in an institution, ascertain why his admission became necessary, whether because of school difficulties, bad conduct, neglect at home, inability to care for himself, or other reasons. When a child is seen in the clinic the problem likewise should be clearly stated. Find out why teachers or parents or other persons wish the child examined. Sometimes the entire trend of examination and inquiry will be determined in accordance with this information. A complete record of the child's past should not be attempted under this heading but chiefly the immediate problem and a general statement of the nature of past difficulties leaving the details for their proper place in the anamnesis.

II. *Family History*—Information pertaining to the various members of the family, especially those in the direct ancestry, should be secured from the point of view of family background and the type of environment which these individuals have created for each other as well as the child who is being studied. It is important to secure an estimate of the family with reference to racial extraction, social and cultural and intellectual level, emotional reactions and prevailing attitudes of members of the family toward one another. This information should be carefully summarized, as well as given in detail for each member of the family. It is well to keep in mind that many problems of an emotional nature encountered in children have their roots somewhere in a faulty organization of the emotional life of the family. The outline for this section of the anamnesis is on pages 17-23.

III. *Personal History*—The personal history should be a chronological record of the child from birth.

The aim of a Personal History is to present a study of the development of the personality including both its assets and liabilities, in conjunction with environmental forces.

In the prenatal period factors which may have had an influence on the vitality and development of the child should be investigated. Such factors may be alcoholism, syphilis, and any serious physical disability which may have contributed to an unfavorable embryonic development. The emotional attitudes of the parents toward the pregnancy may have an influence on later attitudes toward the child.

The birth should be carefully described with special reference to the conditions attending birth, such as prolonged instrumental or difficult labor or any injury done at the time of birth. Convulsions and stupor during the first few days of life and unusual difficulty in establishing respiration may be indications of cerebral birth injury. It is also important to determine whether the birth was full term or premature and the order of birth in relation to siblings, stillbirths and miscarriages should always be given.

For purposes of convenience the first 5 years of life may be regarded as the period of infancy. Inquire if the child was breast or bottle fed, what if any feeding difficulties arose, the details of the interval between feedings, difficulties encountered in weaning, etc. Special attention should be paid to illnesses, surgical operations and accidents during this period of life, giving a careful description of the physical and mental reaction to each on the part of the child and of the parents.

Notations should be made on motor development such as holding the head erect, sitting, crawling, walking, and those on mental development such as alertness to the environment, characteristic inquisitive investigative activity of the infant, development of speech, etc.

As the infant becomes older opportunity is afforded for social integration. It is important to make inquiries as to details of opportunities for social contact with other small children, attitude toward such children, attitude toward play, both individual and collective, etc.

The methods used in training and disciplining small children are of importance and not only the methods themselves but the technique with which they are applied may be of great importance. Somewhat related to these are unusual or special experiences which children may undergo during their infantile period. The experiences may be related to the weaning process, training of bowel and bladder control, sleeping habits, overindulgence and overprotection or too much frustration and too many prohibitions. All of these may condition the child to specific reactions.

The attitudes of parents and others in the immediate family toward the child during the period of infancy should be known. These attitudes may consist of oversolicitude, overconcern, worry, sheltering the child from contacts with children outside the home, inconsistencies of attitudes on the part of the father and mother, etc.

In nearly all problem children one finds even in the period of infancy indications of personality difficulties. Therefore it is important to be on the alert for traits such as tics, enuresis, stammering, vomiting, and any difficult or unusual behavior which may be brought out on careful questioning. Traits and behaviors of these sorts should be described in detail as to setting and circumstances under which they occur.

The period of childhood is ordinarily regarded as beginning at the about the fifth year of life. During this period facts regarding the child's physical condition such as general nutrition, illnesses, accidents, operations, etc., should be described and a careful description obtained of the parents' and child's reactions and attitudes toward these.

His social relationships should be investigated both within and without the family group. Within the family group his attitudes and reactions toward his parents, brothers, and sisters, his reactions to the death of members of the family and to the birth of brothers and sisters should be described. Outside of the family group his attitudes and reactions toward schoolmates, playmates in the neighborhood and teachers should be described. The aim should be to ascertain how successfully he has been able to integrate himself with the social group.

His daily habits, such as hours of sleep, regularity of meals, attitudes and likes or dislikes for food, etc., should be determined. Any unusual behavior should be described in detail as to its setting and circumstances under which it occurs.

His school progress should be noted specifically as this may be a good index to his learning capacity. Hence his progress in school and standing in his class should be given specifically rather than indicated with any general statement. His attitude toward school and toward his lessons with comments on any difficulties in certain school subjects should be given.

The presence of traits such as stammering, tics, enuresis, etc., should be described in detail and the conditions under which they are made worse or are alleviated and their development should be traced in each instance.

During the period of childhood the attitudes of parents and others in the immediate family continue to play an important part in molding the child's personality and conditioning his reactions and building up attitudes of one kind or another.

The outline for the Personal History of the child is on pages 24-28.

Physical Examination

In dealing with children showing psychiatric problems the physical examination is of fundamental value. The physician should approach the physical examination with the idea of determining the general constitutional make-up as well as of ascertaining the presence or absence of some disease process or condition. Detailed instructions and discussion of the physical examination appear on pages 43-54.

Mental Examination

As indicated in the introduction, it is usually not the purpose of the psychiatric examination to disclose a circumscribed set of mental reactions which are sufficiently crystallized to fit them into one or another of the diagnostic groupings used in classifying psychiatric disorders in adults. It is usually therefore not a matter of determining the presence or absence of delusions or hallucinations, dissociated thinking or pathological variations in mood. As a matter of fact such are rarely found. The mental examination aims to secure an understanding of the child's feelings and attitudes toward various experiences, toward various people who contact his life, and toward himself. The psychiatrist must not expect to be able to secure much insight into the child's inner feelings with one or two interviews. The success depends upon the willingness of the child to discuss various intimate topics freely, but more upon the skill and tact of the psychiatrist in fostering the confidence of the child. What is learned through such interviews however can be set forth for purposes of record keeping under the following topical headings:

I. General attitude, conduct and appearance
   1. Attitude toward examiner and examination.
   2. Amount and character of motor activity.
   3. Facial expression, habit movements and general bearing.

II. Stream of mental activity
   1. Productive or underproductive.
   2. Type of response to questions.
   3. Continuity of ideas.
   4. Speech defects, blocking and other abnormalities.

III. Emotional reactions
   1. Tense, inhibited or at ease.
   2. Depressed or elated.
   3. Fearful, shy, timid, natural, uneasy or aggressive.
   4. Excitable.
   5. Ability to establish rapport.
   6. Consistency with ideation.
   7. Other responses.

IV. Mental attitude
   1. Spontaneous account of problems and life history.
   2. Attitude toward home and members of family.
   3. Attitude toward school work, teachers, and pupils.
   4. Attitude toward neighborhood, playmates and play.
   5. Attitude toward self and self-estimation.

Psychometric Examination

Unfortunately the use of psychometric tests has become associated in the minds of many with the diagnosis of mental deficiency. That psychometric tests may indicate a state of mental deficiency is true but they have a far wider use than this. Just as an attempt is made to survey the emotional factors and ideational processes in the child's mind, just so should an attempt be made to survey the child's intellectual capacities. This is done by the use of what is known as a battery of tests. The application and interpretation of psychometric tests by unskilled persons and those not possessed of an adequate training is to be discouraged. They are best made by psychologists who have been particularly trained in this type of work. The tests selected to form the "battery" will depend upon the special features in each case and the judgment of the trained examiner. It is hardly possible to indicate a standard battery of tests but those tests which experience has found to be most useful are listed below.

The Stanford revision of the Binet-Simon test and the Bellevue-Wechsler test are almost universally used and, if administered under favorable conditions, give the level of general intelligence and form a basis for further investigation. They should be regarded as basic tests for use in nearly all cases. For children below 18 months, the Gessell Developmental Schedules or the Infant Intelligence Scale (Psyche Cattell) or several other tests of this type may be used.

In the diagnosis and treatment of some children, a general intelligence test is sufficient to enable the examiner to arrive at a satisfactory psychiatric evaluation of the case. This general test is the very minimum that the examiner should request. In the course of giving this general intelligence test, the psychologist may obtain in addition to the actual intellectual level certain evidence regarding specific personality trends. The particular performance pattern of the child often indicates whether he has any prepsychotic manifestations, organic involvement, or other types of personality deviation. For this reason it is well to require an intelligence test for all the patients.

In many cases, however, much more psychological data need to be on hand before a satisfactory diagnosis can be made and suitable therapy undertaken. Furthermore, many of the children will return to the hospital or clinic at some later date. The existence of psychological data in the case record will be of great assistance in evaluating later problems. Some of the more frequent types of cases which should be referred to the psychologist are:

1. *The child with uneven development.* Some children exhibit such a pattern but it is not unexpected from their particular native endowment. Thus, some children naturally excel in abstract intelligence and are not so gifted in "concrete" intelligence. Such children sometimes are referred as behavior problems or educational problems. The psychologist can help to determine whether the child is suffering from maldevelopment or uneven development by comparing his performance on suitable batteries of tests.

2. *The "dull" child.* Sometimes a child is labeled "dull" when he is actually doing well for his age. The apparent dullness is due to an unusually high level of achievement expected by parents or teachers. By means of educational achievement tests, the child's actual status can be readily determined.

3. *The child who is functioning below his level.* When there is a suspicion that the child is actually functioning below his potential level, the validity of this suspicion can be determined by psychological tests. The cause of this discrepancy, whether it is emotional in character, for example, may sometimes be arrived at by the use of such tests as the Rorschach test, or standardized play techniques.
4. *Specific educational disabilities.* Reading failure accounts for many school problems as well as for much general maladjustment in childhood. Disabilities in arithmetic or other school subjects also serve as sources of difficulty. Special psychological diagnostic tests in the various school subjects are available to the trained psychologist and with their help the existence of the disability can be verified and the type and character of the needed remedial work can be indicated.
5. *Physically handicapped.* Not all the blind and partially blind are necessarily subnormal in intelligence. This holds equally true of the deaf, hard of hearing, and nearly all other physical handicaps. Special intelligence tests are required for each particular type of handicap in order to prevent the specific handicap of the child from affecting his performance on the tests.
6. *Organic involvement.* In some cases there may be a suspicion of some definite organic involvement such as brain injury, tumor, or the general organic picture presented by the postencephalitic child. In all of these cases special psychological tests may help in determining the presence of the organic involvement and its extent.

7. *Convulsive disorders.* Children suffering with convulsive disorders should be tested psychologically as early as possible in order to provide a base-line for evaluating subsequent therapy and personality changes.
8. *Mentally defective.* The presence of mental defect can be readily established in most cases by the Stanford-Binet test or the Bellevue-Wechsler test. For such cases it is often desirable to obtain an estimate of the degree of social maturity exhibited by the patient with the view of determining whether institutionalization is required. The Vineland Social Maturity Scale may be found helpful in this connection. It is also sometimes desirable to determine whether the mental defect is exogenous or endogenous. Certain techniques which the psychologist can readily apply have been evolved for assisting in this determination.

In the evaluation of psychological test results, care must be taken to consider the reliability and validity of the tests. Thus, uncooperative patients often give results which may change markedly on retest when their cooperation is secured. Some tests are by their nature more reliable than others. Thus, the rapidly administered Kent Emergency test is not expected to agree too closely with the results of the more elaborate Stanford-Binet in the case of a given individual child. Even on the same test differences of as much as 5 to 10 points in I. Q. are not unexpected, and even greater changes sometimes occur without necessarily indicating an improvement or deterioration in the patient. In all such instances only a careful evaluation of the test results by the psychologist can throw any light on the condition.

IX

OUTLINE FOR PSYCHIATRIC CASE SUMMARY

The object of a summary is to give a clear, concise and understandable account of all the essential features that go to make up the clinical picture.

In gathering data it is desirable to conform to guides and to arrange the data according to topics but in the *final summary* the order of presentation of the case material will not necessarily follow the guides. The salient features of the case should determine what material is to be included. A good summary is a reflection not only of the interests that the given case may hold, but also of the resourcefulness and conceptions of the physician who has worked with the case.

Summary of the facts. It lends to clarity if the summary begins with a brief statement of what led to the patient's coming under psychiatric observation. The remainder of the summary should be an elaboration, clarification and possible correlation of the outstanding features, so that a clear conception of the influences of those features on the total life reaction may be conveyed.

The data presented should have more than descriptive value; they should have meaning. It often happens that excellent investigations are made, but they lose a good deal of their value because they stand alone, without being correlated.

It is desirable to summarize the case not merely from a descriptive standpoint, but also from the interpretative standpoint, i. e., an effort should be made to trace out the various factors at work and to correlate these with the reaction which the patient shows. Only in this way is it possible to arrive at an *understanding* of the case.

Discussion. This should be an attempt to formulate or interpret the case material under consideration. Much will depend on what the study of the patient has brought out. In general, however, there are certain questions which one should try to answer in the discussion of each case. These may be outlined under the following headings:

(1) *The rôle of heredity and of family influences:* This topic is to be considered not merely from the standpoint of the presence or absence of nervous or mental disorders in the parents or ancestors, but also from the standpoint of the outstanding family traits and characteristics: the family group life, the conflicts, achievements, etc.

(2) *Constitutional factors:* What are the assets and liabilities from the standpoint of constitution? Is the psychological type schizoid or syntoid (introvert or extravert) or mixed? Is the morphological type pyknic, asthenic, athletic or dysplastic?

(3) *Etiological factors:* An attempt should be made to trace the mental and physical factors involved in the breakdown.

A summary of the physical findings should be given. An effort should be made to evaluate the effects of physical diseases, anomalies, defects and injuries on the personality and their bearing on the present mental condition.

A study of the psychogenic causes will usually lead back to early life and requires the consideration of conscious and unconscious tendencies.

(4) *The reaction-type and differential diagnosis:* Discuss whether organic, emotional or trend reaction type and give differential diagnosis.

(5) *Prognosis:* What is the prognosis? What are the favorable and unfavorable features of the reaction?

(6) *Indications for treatment:* What general and special therapeutic measures are indicated?

(7) *Statistical classification:* Classification to be used for statistical report.

X

CLASSIFICATION OF MENTAL DISORDERS

The revised classification is printed below as it appears in the 1942 edition of the Standard Nomenclature of Disease.

It is suggested by the committee that it is desirable that the revised classification be put into effect in all mental hospitals throughout the country. Reports required by the United States Bureau of Census will undoubtedly be based upon it.

Attention is also called to the fact that the condensed form of the classification, which is likewise presented below, may be employed by the mental hospitals for statistical purposes.

MENTAL DISORDERS

00—1 PSYCHOSES DUE TO, OR ASSOCIATED WITH, INFECTION

Record primary physical diagnosis also

0y0-147 Psychoses with syphilis of the central nervous system
- 002-147 Meningo-encephalitic type (general paresis)
- 003-147 Meningo-vascular type (cerebral syphilis)
- 004-147 Psychosis with intracranial gumma
- 0y0-147 Other types. *Specify*

008-123 Psychoses with tuberculous meningitis
008-190 Psychoses with meningitis (unspecified)
003-163 Psychoses with epidemic encephalitis
004-196 Psychoses with acute chorea (Sydenham's)
009-1y0 Psychoses with other infectious disease. *Specify*
009-1xx Post-infectious psychoses. *Specify organism when known (page 62 of the Nomenclature)*

00—3 PSYCHOSES DUE TO INTOXICATION

001-332 Psychoses due to alcohol
- 002-332 Pathologic intoxication
- 003-332 Delirium tremens
- 004-332 Korsakoff's psychosis
- 007-332 Acute hallucinosis
- 0y0-332 Other types. *Specify*

Code numbers are those used in "A Standard Nomenclature of Disease," prepared by the National Conference on Medical Nomenclature, published by the American Medical Association, Chicago.

*y signifies an incomplete diagnosis. It is to be replaced, whenever possible, by a code digit signifying specific diagnosis.

002-300 Psychoses due to a drug or other exogenous poison
002-310 Psychoses due to a metal. *Specify* (*page* 70 *of the Nomenclature*)
002-350 Psychoses due to a gas. *Specify* (*page* 72 *of the Nomenclature*)
002-370 Psychoses due to opium or a derivative
002-3.. Psychoses due to another drug. *Specify* (*page* 70 *of the Nomenclature*)

00—4 PSYCHOSES DUE TO TRAUMA (TRAUMATIC PSYCHOSES)

009-42x Delirium due to trauma
009-4x9 Personality disorders due to trauma
003-4xx Mental deterioration due to trauma
003-4y0 Other types. *Specify*

00—5.0 PSYCHOSES DUE TO DISTURBANCE OF CIRCULATION

Record primary physical diagnosis also

003-512 Psychoses with cerebral embolism
003-516 Psychoses with cerebral arteriosclerosis
009-5xx Psychoses with cardiorenal disease
003-5y0 Other types. *Specify*

00—5.5 PSYCHOSES DUE TO CONVULSIVE DISORDER (EPILEPSY)

003-550 Epileptic deterioration
003-560 Epileptic clouded states
003-5y5 Other epileptic types. *Specify.*

00—7 PSYCHOSES DUE TO DISTURBANCES OF METABOLISM, GROWTH, NUTRITION OR ENDOCRINE FUNCTION

Record primary physical diagnosis also

001-79x Senile psychoses
002-79x Simple deterioration
003-79x Presbyophrenic type
004-79x Delirious and confused types
005-79x Depressed and agitated types
006-79x Paranoid types
930-796 Presenile sclerosis (Alzheimer's disease)
001-796 Involutional psychoses
002-796 Melancholia
003-796 Paranoid types
0y0-796 Other types. *Specify*
00x-770 Psychoses with glandular disorder. *Specify glandular disorder* (*page* 442 *of the Nomenclature*)
009-712 Exhaustion delirium
009-7623 Psychoses with pellagra
009-yxx Psychoses with other somatic disease. *Specify disease*

00—8 PSYCHOSES DUE TO NEW GROWTH

Record primary diagnosis

003-8.. Psychoses with intracranial neoplasm. *Specify* (*page* 87 *of the Nomenclature*)

009-8.. Psychoses with other neoplasm. *Specify* (*page* 87 *of the Nomenclature*)

00—9 PSYCHOSES DUE TO UNKNOWN OR HEREDITARY CAUSE BUT ASSOCIATED WITH ORGANIC CHANGE

Record primary physical diagnosis also

006-953 Psychoses with multiple sclerosis

004-953 Psychoses with paralysis agitans

004-992 Psychoses with Huntington's chorea

004-9y0 Psychoses with other disease of the brain or nervous system. *Specify disease*

00—X DISORDERS OF PSYCHOGENIC ORIGIN OR WITHOUT CLEARLY DEFINED TANGIBLE CAUSE OR STRUCTURAL CHANGE

001-x10 Manic-depressive psychoses

- 001-x11 Manic type
- 001-x12 Depressive type
- 001-x13 Circular type
- 001-x14 Mixed type
- 001-x15 Perplexed type
- 001-x16 Stuporous type
- 001-x1y Other types. *Specify*

001-x20 Dementia præcox (schizophrenia)

- 001-x21 Simple type
- 001-x22 Hebephrenic type
- 001-x23 Catatonic type
- 001-x24 Paranoid type
- 001-x20 Other types. *Specify*

001-x30 Paranoia

001-x31 Paranoid conditions

001-x40 Psychoses with psychopathic personality

001-x50 Psychoses with mental deficiency[1]

1. For patients over 16 years specify mental level as idiot, imbecile or moron; intelligence quotient (I. Q.) based on 16 year level.

Psychoneuroses

See also under organ (*Category* 5.5)

Hysteria

002-x00 Anxiety hysteria

002-x10 Conversion hysteria

002-x11 Anesthetic type. *Indicate symptomatic manifestations (page* 508 *of the Nomenclature), e.g.:* x12 amaurosis, x06 deafness, 55x anesthesia of . . ., x41 anosmia

002-x12 Paralytic type. *Indicate symptomatic manifestations (page* 508), *e.g.:* 561 monoplegia, 563 hemiplegia, x32 ophthalmoplegia, 956 aphonia

002-x13 Hyperkinetic type. *Indicate symptomatic manifestations (page* 508), *e.g.,* 225 tic (facial or other), 222 spasm, 228 tremor, 20x postures, 936 catalepsy, 934 convulsions, 302 stammering, 301 stuttering

002-x14 Paresthetic type. *Indicate symptomatic manifestations (page* 508), *e.g.:* 506 dysesthesia, 507 paresthesia

002-x15 Autonomic type. *Indicate symptomatic manifestations (page* 508), *e.g.:* 154 hyperhidrosis, 153 edema, 159 ulceration

002-x16 Amnesic type. *Indicate symptomatic manifestations (page* 508 *of the Nomenclature), e.g.:* 901 fugue, 911 amnesia, 917 somnambulism, 936 catalepsy, 902 trance, 903 dissociated personality, 931 delirium, x07 hallucination of hearing, 904 dream states, 933 stupor

002-x1x Mixed hysterical psychoneurosis. *Indicate symptomatic combinations by using the various symptoms included under the different types in this section or those listed on page* 488

Psychasthenia or compulsive states

002-x21 Obsession. *Indicate symptomatic manifestations (page* 488) *e.g.:* 905 delire de toucher, 906 counting (steps, etc), 908 urge to say words, 971 kleptomania, 974 dipsomania, 972 pyromania, 973 trichotillomania, 907 folie du doute.

002-x22 Compulsive tics and spasms. *Indicate symptomatic manifestations (page* 488), *e.g.:* 228 tremor, 227 occupation spasm or tic, 226 habit spasm or tic, 224 spasmus nutans, 301 stuttering, 302 stammering

002-x23 Phobia. *Indicate symptomatic manifestations (page* 488) *e.g.:* 983 claustrophobia, 984 syphilophobia, 985 agoraphobia, 986 misophobia.

002-x2x Mixed compulsive states. *Indicate symptomatic combinations by using the various symptoms included under the different types in this section or those listed on page* 508 *of the Nomenclature*

002-x30 Neurasthenia

002-x31 Hypochondriasis

002-x32 Reactive depression (simple situational reaction, or other type)

002-x33 Anxiety state

002-x34 Anorexia nervosa

002-x0x Mixed psychoneurosis. *Indicate symptomatic combinations by using the various symptoms included in this section or those listed on page* 508 *ff.:* 981 anxiety, 982 depression, 0x0 fatigue.

001-y00 Undiagnosed psychoses

0y0-y00 Without mental disorder. *Diagnosis to be used in psychiatric clinics. Also in psychiatric and psychopathic hospitals, to account for patients submitted for observation or allowed to remain in hospital for other legitimate reason. Record condition also in positive terms, as*

930-yxx Epilepsy

000-332 Alcoholism

000-3xx Drug addiction

00-yxx Mental deficiency[1]

000-163 Disorders of personality due to epidemic encephalitis

000-x40 Psychopathic personality

000-x41 With pathologic sexuality. *Indicate symptomatic manifestations (page* 508 *of the Nomenclature), e.g.:* 991 homosexuality, 992 erotomania, 993 sexual perversion, 994 sexual immaturity

000-x42 With pathologic emotionality. *Indicate symptomatic manifestations (page* 508), *e.g.:* 041 schizoid personality, 042 cyclothmic personality, 913 paranoid personality, 043 emotional instability

000-x43 With asocial or amoral trends. *Indicate symptomatic manifestations (page* 508) *e.g.:* 044 antisocialism, 047 pathologic mendacity, 046 moral deficiency, 048 vagabondage, 987 misanthropy

000-x4x Mixed types. *Indicate symptomatic manifestations by using the various symptoms included under the different types in this section or those listed on page* 508

0y0-y05 Other nonpsychotic diseases or conditions. *Specify. Use this term for statistical purposes only; diagnose each disease in specific terms according to appropriate section of Nomenclature*

Primary Behavior Disorders

000-x61 Simple adult maladjustment

Primary behavior disorders in children

000-x71 Habit disturbance. *Indicate symptomatic manifestations (page* 508), *e.g.:* 031 nail biting, 032 thumb sucking, 722 enuresis, 034 masturbation, 033 tantrums

000-x72 Conduct disturbance. *Indicate symptomatic manifestations (page* 508 *of the Nomenclature), e.g.:* 04x truancy, 050 quarrelsomeness, 051 disobedience, 059 untruthfulness, 054 stealing, 055 forgery, 056 setting fires, 053 destructiveness, 057 use of alcohol, 058 use of drugs, 052 cruelty, 995 sex offenses, 049 vagrancy

000-x73 Neurotic traits. *Indicate symptomatic manifestations (page* 508), *e.g.:* 225 tics, 226 habit spasm, 917 somnambulism, 302 stammering, 006 overactivity, 980 fears

1. For patients over 16 years specify mental level as idiot, imbecile or moron; intelligence quotient (I. Q.) based on 16 year level.

Condensed Form of New Classification as Approved by the Council of the American Psychiatric Association

As it is clearly impracticable to use the complete classification of mental disorders in statistical tables, the following condensed classification has been arranged for statistical purposes.

For complete diagnosis for use in case records or for research purposes, it is recommended that the detailed classification be used.

Condensed Classification of Mental Disorders

01 Psychoses with syphilitic meningo-encephalitis (general paresis).

02 Psychoses with other forms of syphilis of the central nervous system.

- 021 Meningo-vascular type (cerebral syphilis).
- 022 With intracranial gumma.
- 023 Other types.

03 Psychoses with epidemic encephalitis.

04 Psychoses with other infectious diseases.

- 041 With tuberculous meningitis.
- 042 With meningitis (unspecified).
- 043 With acute chorea (Sydenham's).
- 044 With other infectious disease.
- 045 Post-infectious psychoses.

05 Psychoses due to alcohol.

- 051 Pathological intoxication.
- 052 Delirium tremens.
- 053 Korsakoff's psychosis.
- 054 Acute hallucinosis.
- 055 Other types.

06 Psychoses due to a drug or other exogenous poison.

- 061 Due to a metal
- 062 Due to a gas.
- 063 Due to opium or a derivative.
- 064 Due to another drug.

07 Psychoses due to trauma.

- 071 Delirium due to trauma.
- 072 Personality disorder due to trauma.
- 073 Mental deterioration due to trauma.
- 074 Other types.

08 Psychoses with cerebral arteriosclerosis.

09 Psychoses with other disturbances of circulation.

091 With cerebral embolism.
092 With cardio-renal disease.
093 Other types.

10 Psychoses due to convulsive disorder (epilepsy).

101 Epileptic deterioration.
102 Epileptic clouded states.
103 Other epileptic types.

11 Senile psychoses.

111 Simple deterioration.
112 Presbyophrenic type.
113 Delirious and confused types.
114 Depressed and agitated types.
115 Paranoid types.

12 Involutional psychoses.

121 Melancholia.
122 Paranoid types.
123 Other types.

13 Psychoses due to other metabolic, etc., diseases.

131 With glandular disorder.
132 Exhaustion delirium.
133 Alzheimer's disease (presenile sclerosis).
134 With pellagra.
135 With other somatic disease.

14 Psychoses due to new growth.

141 With intracranial neoplasm.
142 With other neoplasms.

15 Psychoses due to unknown or hereditary cause but associated with organic change.

151 With multiple sclerosis.
152 With paralysis agitans.
153 With Huntington's chorea.
154 With other disease of the brain or nervous system.

16 Psychoneuroses.

161 Hysteria (anxiety hysteria, conversion hysteria and subgroups).
162 Psychasthenia or compulsive states (and subgroups).
163 Neurasthenia.
164 Hypochondriasis.
165 Reactive depression (simple situational reaction, others).
166 Anxiety state.
167 Anorexia nervosa.
168 Mixed psychoneurosis.

17 Manic-depressive psychoses.

- 171 Manic type.
- 172 Depressive type.
- 173 Circular type.
- 174 Mixed type.
- 175 Perplexed type.
- 176 Stuporous type.
- 177 Other types.

18 Dementia praecox (schizophrenia).

- 181 Simple type.
- 182 Hebephrenic type.
- 183 Catatonic type.
- 184 Paranoid type.
- 185 Other types.

19 Paranoia and paranoid conditions.

- 191 Paranoia.
- 192 Paranoid conditions.

20 Psychoses with psychopathic personality.

21 Psychoses with mental deficiency.

22 Undiagnosed psychoses.

23 Without mental disorder.

- 231 Epilepsy.
- 232 Alcoholism.
- 233 Drug addiction.
- 234 Mental deficiency.
- 235 Disorders of personality due to epidemic encephalitis.
- 236 Psychopathic personality.
  - 2361 With pathologic sexuality.
  - 2362 With pathologic emotionality.
  - 2363 With asocial or amoral trends.
  - 2364 Mixed types.
- 237 Other nonpsychotic diseases or conditions.

24 Primary behavior disorders.

- 241 Simple adult maladjustment.
- 242 Primary behavior disorders in children.
  - 2421 Habit disturbance.
  - 2422 Conduct disturbance.
  - 2423 Neurotic traits.

DEFINITIONS AND EXPLANATORY NOTES

00-1 *Psychoses due to or associated with infection*

0y0-147 Psychoses with syphilis of the central nervous system

It is expected that cases shall be classified as far as possible under the sub-groups (002, 003, 004, 00y). A classification under this general heading is to be made only after failure of every reasonable effort to determine the predominating pathological process.

002-147 Meningo-encephalitic types (general paresis)

The earlier clinically descriptive term, general paralysis, has been discarded in the present classification for the term indicating the fundamental pathological process. Under this heading are to be classified cases showing rapidly or slowly progressive organic intellectual and emotional defects with physical signs and symptoms of parenchymatous syphilis of the nervous system and completely positive serology, including the paretic gold curve. Cases showing symptoms suggestive of manic-depressive, dementia præcox or of other constitutional psychotic reactions, but showing also physical signs and symptoms of syphilis of the nervous system and positive serology, particularly the paretic gold curve, are to be listed here rather than under other headings. It is to be remembered that with the modern methods of treatment a number of paretics may be found with altered or even negative serology. Here the history, particularly that of the length and nature of treatment, must be taken into consideration in making the final classification.

003-147 Meningo-vascular type (cerebral syphilis)

Under this heading are to be classified cases in which the history, signs and symptoms, including serology point to a primary and predominating involvement of the meninges and blood vessels rather than of the parenchyma of the nervous system. Indicating cerebral syphilis rather than paresis are: comparatively early onset after infection, sudden onset with confusion or delirium, focal signs, particularly cranial nerve palsies, apoplectiform seizures, very high spinal fluid cell count, positive blood Wassermann and negative spinal fluid Wassermann and the luetic type of gold curve, often prompt response to systemic antisyphilitic treatment. Under this heading are also to be classified those cases of chronic syphilitic meningitis which may show mild or severe deterioration in emotional and intellectual reactions, but which usually nevertheless show a clinical picture distinguishable from the paretic. Cases showing psychotic reactions on a basis of cerebral lesions from vascular disease determined to be of a syphilitic nature should be classified here rather than under the heading of "Psychoses due to disturbances of the circulation." The determination of the syphilitic nature of the vascular disease may be difficult in these old "burned out" cases of syphilis as the serology may be entirely negative. A history of syphilis, of its treatment, of vascular attacks earlier in life, and signs of old systemic syphilis help in the differentiation.

004-147 Psychoses with intracranial gumma

Under this heading are to be classified those comparatively rare cases in which the predominating pathological process is gummatous formation, either single or multiple. In most cases gummata are a part of a diffuse meningo-vascular process under which they should be classified. Occasionally solitary gumma of large size occur, giving the symptoms of intracranial pressure with or without focal signs. Serological examination helps to differentiate these from other intracranial growths. It is to be remembered that persons with systemic syphilis may have brain tumors, and that a positive blood Wassermann in the presence of signs of intracranial growth does not necessarily indicate a gumma. Spinal fluid examination is necessary. Response to antisyphilitic treatment may help in the classification.

0y0-147 Other types (to be specified)

Here should be classified the comparatively infrequent cases of psychoses with syphilis of the central nervous system not covered in the above mentioned groups, including psychoses with tabes dorsalis, providing it is determined that such cases do not belong in the paretic group or the group of cerebral syphilis, as they frequently do. Psychoses ascribed to or associated with syphilitic meningo-myelitis may be placed here, with the same reservations.

008-123 Psychoses with tuberculous meningitis

Psychoses developing during the course of a demonstrated tuberculous meningitis should be reported here. Cases developing a tuberculous meningitis during the course of a psychosis should not be reported under this heading but under the primary psychoses.

008-190 Psychoses with meningitis (unspecified)

Here are to be classified those cases developing meningitis, the type of which cannot be specified. Psychoses associated with other forms of meningitis which can be specifically determined are to be listed elsewhere under their proper headings.

003-163 Psychoses with epidemic encephalitis

Here are to be listed those mental disturbances associated with acute phases of epidemic encephalitis such as delirium, drowsiness, or stupor with fever and muscnlar twitchings, and those chronic cases with demonstrable residual defects of the intellectual processes and emotions. These defects show themselves in a diminution of voluntary attention, of spontaneous interest, and of initiative; memory impairment is often slight. Instability, apathy, depression, euphoria, anxiety, and anti-social reactions may be found from case to case. Many patients are of the parkinsonian type with mental reactions resembling schizophrenia; often the whole personality is disorganized.

004-196 Psychoses with acute chorea (Sydenham's)

Here are to be classified patients showing acute and chronic mental disturbances associated with Sydenham's chorea, which may be associated with a more or less marked encephalopathy. Care should be taken to distinguish this type of chorea from the hysterical type; in differentiating, a history of rheumatism and repeated attacks of tonsillitis, presence of cardiac disease, and fever help in the establishment of the diagnosis of Sydenham's chorea.

009-1y0 Psychoses with other infectious disease (to be specified)

Here are to be classified those psychoses which are primarily and predominantly to be ascribed to, or associated with, infectious disease particularly during the febrile period. The most common clinical picture met is that of delirium with or without motor excitement or hallucinations. There are frequent shifts in the levels of consciousness; the attacks may be followed by amnesia for the period. These infectious psychoses are particularly apt to arise in association with influenza, pneumonia, typhoid fever and acute articular rheumatism. In the classification, care should be taken to distinguish between these infectious psychoses and other psychoses, particularly the manic-depressive and dementia præcox reactions, which may be made manifest by even a mild attack of infectious disease. Delirious reactions occurring in connection with childbirth are not to be looked upon as infectious psychoses unless there is clear-cut evidence of infection with toxemia, so that the infection appears to be the main etiological factor.

009-1xx Post-infectious psychoses (infection to be specified)

Here are to be classified those mental disturbances arising during the post-febrile period or the period of convalescence from infectious disease, frequently showing themselves as mild forms of confusion, or depressive, irritable, suspicious reactions. Here also are to be classified the occasionally occurring states of mental enfeeblement following acute infectious disease, especially typhoid fever, acute articular rheumatism, and meningitis. Abnormal mental states arising as part of the asthenia or exhaustion following infectious disease are to be classified here rather than under the heading of exhaustion delirium.

00-3 *Psychoses due to intoxication*

001-332 Psychoses due to alcohol

Under this heading are to be grouped only those cases that have abnormal mental reactions which can reasonably be concluded to have alcohol as the main etiological factor. Excessive alcoholism may be a symptom of some other psychosis or psychopathological condition or, on the other hand, it may aggravate and bring to notice an already-existing psychosis of a non-alcoholic nature. Such cases are to be carefully distinguished by the previous history, by the symptomatology and course, and should be grouped elsewhere under their proper categories.

002-332 Pathological intoxication

Under this heading belong those cases which show as a result of small or large amounts of alcohol sudden excitation or twilight states, often with a mistaking of the situation and also with illusions and hallucinations and marked emotional reactions, particularly of anxiety or rage. Such an attack may last a few minutes or a number of hours and usually there is complete amnesia for the attack. In making such a classification epileptic conditions precipitated by small amounts of alcohol, or catatonic excitation in dementia præcox or manic-depressive reactions or general paresis or arteriosclerotic episodes are to be ruled out.

003-332 Delirium tremens

Little difficulty is usually experienced in reaching a classification in a case of delirium tremens; the delirium, often of sudden onset but frequently showing premonitory signs of nervousness and "jumpiness," with predominantly visual and tactile hallucinations and distinct clouding of the sensorium, defects of attention and physical prostration, with marked tremors, point to this classification. The visual hallucinations are commonly zooscopic in type; the tactile, of crawling insects; the auditory, of threats and criticisms, are not numerous. The combined experiences cause active fear and acute excitement. This type of delirium may pass on into Korsakoff's psychosis or other chronic reactions.

004-332 Korsakoff's psychosis

This reaction is sometimes referred to as chronic alcoholic delirium in contrast to the acute delirium of delirium tremens. The onset of the two types of reactions may be similar although in the Korsakoff reaction there is noticed at times a more marked interference with the intellectual functions than in delirium tremens. The course is a protracted one, however. After the acute stages are recovered from, there is usually a striking defect of retention with confabulation. Perhaps the majority of these patients are left with a permanent defect of memory and retention but occasionally patients are seen who completely recover. Polyneuritis is frequently a part of the total reaction; it may be severe leaving physical defects of a permanent nature; in other cases it is slight and is recovered from, and in still other cases polyneuritis is not demonstrable and is not considered necessarily a criterion of the Korsakoff reaction. The Korsakoff syndrome appearing in connection with other toxic conditions, i. e., toxemia in pregnancy, should not be classified under this heading.

007-332 Acute hallucinosis

Under this heading should be grouped those cases that as a result of the excessive use of alcohol develop hallucinations suddenly or gradually, particularly of the auditory type with derogatory content causing a characteristic fear or anxiety reaction but with retention of clearness of the sensorium. Physical prostration and other toxic physical signs are not as outstanding as they are in delirium tremens. These cases, particularly those which do not recover within a few weeks but continue in a chronic hallucinatory state, often require careful differentiation from dementia præcox reactions and consideration has to be given to the possibility that in certain potential or actual cases of dementia præcox alcohol has precipitated a psychotic reaction which should be classified as one fundamentally of dementia præcox.

0y0-332 Other types (to be specified)

Under this heading are to be grouped psychotic reactions on an alcoholic basis not already specified in the above sub-groups. In the present sub-group there may be placed under the designation "Deterioration," those chronic alcoholics who appear to show deterioration not only in the moral and ethical senses and in their emotional blunting, but also evidence of an organic memory defect. Alcoholic "pseudoparesis" belongs in this group. Other chronic alcoholics who seem to develop paranoid ideas, particularly delusions of infidelity in connection with chronic drinking, may best be placed in this sub-group with the designation "Paranoid type."

002-300 Psychoses due to a drug or other exogenous poison

002-310 Psychoses due to a metal (to be specified)

Here are to be grouped those psychotic cases due usually to prolonged exposure to metallic poisoning, particularly lead, arsenic and mercury. Persons so exposed, often showing earlier gastrointestinal and peripheral nerve toxic symptoms, may develop deliria with marked prostration from which they may recover or they may be left with intellectual or emotional defects apparently based on encephalopathy associated with these toxic conditions. The clinical picture at times resembles the Korsakoff mental state.

002-350 Psychoses due to a gas

Under this heading should be placed the cases that develop mental disturbance from exposure to poisonous gases, particularly carbon monoxide gas in illuminating gas and automobile exhaust. The preliminary period of unconsciousness may be followed by a more or less protracted delirium after which the patients may be left with increased fatigability and difficulty in concentration. It should be recalled that persons who have suffered from carbon monoxide poisoning may appear to clear up entirely from the initial disturbance and have a free interval lasting over weeks, to be followed by the appearance of symptoms of defect which may not be recovered from. These patients remain in a chronic state of mild or severe mental enfeeblement, due to special lesions produced in the brain.

002-370 Psychoses due to opium or a derivative

Here should be grouped those comparatively infrequent psychotic reactions appearing in habitual users of opium and particularly its derivative, morphine. Such effects appear to show themselves in mental deterioration with demonstrable memory defect as well as ethical and social deterioration. Occasionally visual hallucinations are noted. Paranoid states may also develop. Difficulty may be experienced in differentiating the actual effects of the morphine intoxication from the underlying personality defects which seem frequently to be present and which would place these individuals for statistical purposes rather in the group of psychopathic personalities. Drug addicts who do not show definite psychotic manifestations sufficiently to justify their hospitalization or their special treatment because of their mental condition should be classified not under this sub-group but under the heading drug addiction (000-3xx).

002-3.. Psychoses due to another drug

Here should be classified those cases which develop abnormal mental states in association with long continued or brief excessive use of other drugs such as cocaine, bromides, chloral, atropine, marihuana, acetanilide, phenacetin, sulphonal, trional and proprietary combinations. Following the use of these drugs certain individuals may become dull or apathetic, these conditions sometimes being followed by toxic delirium with confusion, hallucination of sight and hearing, flight of of ideas, confabulation, misidentification and paraphasia. Cases developing a toxic reaction from the use of drugs in the treatment of another form of psychosis should be reported according to the primary psychosis and not as drug psychoses.

00-4 *Psychoses due to trauma* (*traumatic psychoses*)

Under this heading should be classified only those cases of fairly characteristic psychotic reactions which it is reasonable to conclude were brought about by head or brain injury as a result of force directly or indirectly applied to the head. Psychoses following injuries to other parts of the body are not to be classified here. Manic-depressive psychoses, general paresis, dementia præcox and psychoneuroses in which trauma may act as a contributing or precipitating cause should not be included in this group.

009-42x Delirium due to trauma

Here belong those cases of acute (concussion) delirium developing immediately following head injury with or without an alcoholic or senile background, and also those which show following such injury a protracted or chronic delirium which often resembles the Korsakoff syndrome, with superficial alertness but marked disorientation, memory defect and confabulations.

009-4x9 Personality disorders due to trauma

This term is used in place of the former designation of posttraumatic constitution and is intended to apply to those cases showing posttraumatic changes in disposition, with vasomotor instability, headache, fatigability and explosive emotional reactions, amnesic hysterical states, intolerance to alcohol, and sometimes convulsive or hysterical seizures, or paranoid developments. A complete history of the previous personality reactions and a careful evaluation of the present reaction are often necessary to rule out psychoneuroses.

003-4xx Mental deterioration due to trauma

Here are to be classified those cases which, following severe or apparently slight head injury with or without an acute or protracted delirium, develop gradually mental enfeeblement or terminal deterioration. Symptoms mentioned under posttraumatic personality disorders may also be present. Psychoses to be ascribed to arteriosclerosis, complicated by head injury, may be difficult to differentiate. If the case history shows symptoms of arteriosclerosis before the injury and the mental and physical examination bears this out the case should be classified under that heading instead of under the present one. It is to be remembered that the confusion of an arteriosclerotic or a cerebral attack may have brought about the head injury.

003-4y0 Other types (to be specified)

It appears that only occasionally will other traumatic reaction types be found to be classified under this heading.

00-5.0 *Psychoses due to disturbance of circulation*

003-512 Psychoses with cerebral embolism

Emboli interfering with the cerebral circulation, causing cerebral softening and neurological or psychotic symptoms, may arise from the pulmonary circulation, from vegetations on the heart valves or from thrombosis of the arteries of the neck and head. The incidence of such occurrences is comparatively rare, however.

003-516 Psychoses with cerebral arteriosclerosis

Here are classified the comparatively large group of middle-aged and old persons who show evidence of interference with the cerebral circulation in such symptoms as difficulty in sustained mental operations, confusion, loss of memory and general impairment of the intellectual functions in varying degrees. Preservation of the personality and insight into the defects may be present in early or mild cases but in severe circulatory disturbance, with cerebral destruction, mental enfeeblement may be advanced to a high degree. In elderly persons hypertension may or may not be found in the presence of severe vascular disease. Cases with essential hypertension or with arteriosclerosis without demonstrable degenerative changes in the larger vessels but showing psychotic symptoms of the arteriosclerotic type should be classified here. Differentiation from the senile psychoses is sometimes difficult; the pathological changes lying at the basis of the two psychotic reaction types may be associated. Periodic remissions of the symptoms are more often seen in arteriosclerosis than in senile deterioration. The age, history, and careful survey of the symptoms often assist one in determining which is the predominant type of reaction, but where such a determination is not clearly possible, preference should continue to be given, for statistical purposes, to the arteriosclerotic classification.

009-5xx Psychoses with cardiorenal disease

Here are to be classified those psychotic disturbances, particularly deliria or temporary periods of confusion, often worse at night, shown by persons with cardiac disease, especially in stages of decompensation. Fearful hallucinations sometimes occur. There is difficulty in concentration, and memory may be impaired. Marked fluctuations in the degree of mental clearness may be striking; depression, futility, panic states, and paranoid streaks are not uncommon. Also to be classified here are the psychotic changes associated with acute and chronic kidney disease, including uremia.

003-5y0 Other types (to be specified)

Rarely will there be psychoses developing because of disturbance of circulation that may not be properly classified under the headings already mentioned but if such cases arise they should be classified under the present heading.

00-5.5 *Psychoses due to convulsive disorder (epilepsy)*

Under this heading will be classified only cases that show psychotic disturbances in connection with epilepsy which appears to be primary, essential, or idiopathic. Cases showing convulsive manifestations symptomatic of other diseases are to be classified under the headings for these diseases rather than under the present heading.

003-550 Epileptic deterioration

Under this heading are to be classified those epileptics who show a gradual development of mental dullness, slowness of association and thinking, impairment of memory, irritability or apathy. Various accessory symptoms, paranoid delusions and hallucinations may be added to this fundamental deterioration.

003-560 Epileptic clouded states

Here are to be classified those epileptics who develop preceding or following convulsive attacks or, as equivalents of attacks, dazed reactions with deep confusion, bewilderment and anxiety or excitement, with hallucinations, fears and violent outbreaks; instead of fear there may be ecstatic moods with religious exaltation.

003-5y5 Other epileptic types

Here are to be classified the occasional epileptics who without obvious deterioration or clouded states may develop psychotic manifestations such as paranoid trends or hallucinatory states, depressions or elations. The type resembling schizophrenia or having schizophrenic features should be placed here statistically.

00-7 *Psychoses due to disturbance of metabolism, growth, nutrition or endocrine function*

001-79x Senile psychoses

Some feebleness of mind is characteristic of and normal for old age. It may be designated as senility or dotage. It is characterized by self-centering of interests, reminiscence, and difficulty in assimilation of new experiences so that there is forgetfulness of recent occurrences; childish emotional reactions are prominent, with irritability aroused on slight provocation. Such mental states may best be classified under a heading "Senility" in the group "Without psychoses," rather than with the senile psychoses. The following senile psychoses are characterized pathologically by various degrees of atrophy of the cerebral cortex, loss of ganglion cells, gliosis, and "plaque" formation.

002-79x Simple deterioration

Under this heading should be classified as psychotic those persons who show definite exaggeration of the normal senile mental change in loss of memory for recent events particularly, defects of attention and concentration, misidentification of persons and of places and lack of appreciation of time. Such persons may require special hospital care because of restless wandering, marked irritability or assaultiveness, erotic excitement or because of delusions which may be fleeting or persistent. Deterioration of the mental processes may progress to a state of vegetative existence.

003-79x Presbyophrenic type

Under this heading are to be classified those cases of senile psychosis showing severe memory and retention defects with complete disorientation but at the same time preservation of mental alertness and attentiveness with ability to grasp immediate impressions and conversation quite well. Forgetfulness leads to marked contradictions and repetitions; suggestibility and free fabrication are prominent symptoms. The general picture resembles the Korsakoff mental complex.

004-79x Delirious and confused types

Here are to be classified those cases in which the outstanding picture is one of deep confusion or of a delirious condition. This type of reaction is often precipitated by acute illness.

005-79x Depressed and agitated types

In certain cases of senile psychoses the outstanding picture may be one of pronounced depressions and persistent agitation. Such patients are to be distinguished from cases of involution melancholia by the presence of fundamental defects of the memory and grasp of recent occurrences.

006-79x Paranoid types

In certain cases well-marked delusional trends, chiefly of a persecutory or expansive nature may accompany the deterioration; in the early stages the diagnosis may be difficult particularly if the defect symptoms are mild or absent on superficial examination.

930-796 Presenile sclerosis (Alzheimer's disease)

This condition is characterized in its pathological manifestations by a very marked brain atrophy with microscopic focal necroses and neurofibral alteration. Clinically these cases present at a comparatively early age period, sometimes in the forties, a high degree of dementia, often with aphasic or apractic symptoms. In the absence of other causes for an organic dementia Alzheimer's disease is to be considered, although few cases may be classified clinically as belonging to this group. Pick's disease probably belongs here also.

001-796 Involutional psychoses

002-796 Melancholia

Here are to be classified the depressions occurring in middle life and later years without evidence of organic intellectual defects, characterized mainly by agitation, uneasiness and insomnia, often with self-condemnatory trends. For statistical purposes, cases showing such symptoms but with a history of previous attacks of depression or excitement should be classified with the manic-depressive group.

003-796 Paranoid types

Here should be classified those cases which during the involutional period, and without previous indication of paranoid reaction, show transitory or prolonged paranoid reactions with delusions of persecution, suspiciousness and misinterpretation.

0y0-796 Other types (to be specified)

Other types of psychotic reactions occurring during the involutional period and from which organic brain disease can be excluded, may be classified under this heading.

00x-770 Psychoses with glandular disorder (to be specified)

This classification is provided for those cases which show psychoses obviously to be ascribed to diseases of the endocrine glands, separating them off for statistical purposes from psychoses occurring with other somatic diseases. Outstanding among the cases classified here are psychoses associated with disorders of the function of the thyroid gland, more specifically the hallucinatory deliria of thyroidtoxicosis and the apathy of myxoedema, the latter often accompanied by paranoid trends. Psychoses to be ascribed to diabetes, disorders of the pituitary, Addison's disease and multiglandular disorders should be classified under this heading.

009-712 Exhaustion delirium

Under this heading should be classified only those cases which do not have infectious disease or other organic disease as a basis for the delirium. Exhaustion probably plays a restricted rôle in etiology, excepting under very unusual conditions. It may appear as the aftermath of a long and debilitating infectious disease like enteric fever, or from extreme exposure or hardship, or from prolonged emotional conflicts. Care should also be taken to rule out manic-depressive and dementia præcox reactions of a delirious nature before classifying cases as due to exhaustion. With proper elimination of cases belonging to the other categories it appears that cases with true exhaustion delirium are rare.

009-7623 Psychoses with pellagra

Under this heading should be classified only those psychoses developing during the course of pellagra and apparently caused by this disease. The mental disturbances occurring in connection with pellagra are deliria or confused states similar to other toxic-organic reactions. Depressions are common and the "central neuritis" reaction described by Adolf Meyer is encountered in many cases. Cases developing pellagra during the course of some other psychosis should not be classified under this heading but rather under the primary psychosis.

009-yxx Psychoses with other somatic disease (to be specified)

Here should be classified only those psychoses developing in connection with other somatic disease not already specified in the classification, ruling out psychoses with infectious diseases and postinfectious psychoses which are provided for elsewhere in the classification.

00-8 *Psychoses due to new growth*

003-8.. Psychoses with intracranial neoplasm

Psychoses developing during the course of intracranial neoplasms (brain tumor) should be classified here whether the brain tumor is primary or secondary.

009-8.. Psychoses with other neoplasm

Here should be classified those psychoses developing in connection with new growth elsewhere in the body, these growths being instrumental in bringing about psychotic reactions either by their general toxic effects or by their psychological effects on the patient. Toxic delirious conditions may be seen or depressions with hopelessness, with or without agitation.

00-9 *Psychoses due to unknown or hereditary causes, but associated with organic changes*

Under this heading, which takes the place of the former classification designation of "Psychoses with other brain and nervous diseases," are to be classified those psychoses developing with, and as a part of, certain diseases of the nervous system not classified under foregoing headings, specifically multiple sclerosis, paralysis agitans, and Huntington's chorea. These psychoses are essentially of the organic brain disease type, with defects in the intellectual functions and emotional deterioration, sometimes with accessory symptoms of hallucinations and delusions. Cases showing psychoses of a constitutional or functional nature prior to the development of symptoms of the organic nervous disease, and in which therefore the latter disease seems incidental, should be grouped under the heading of the primary psychosis rather than under the present heading.

00-X *Disorders of psychogenic origin or without clearly defined tangible cause or structural change*

This heading is so worded in the present nomenclature to imply that the disorders classified under it may or may not be of psychogenic origin, but that there is no *clearly defined tangible* cause or structural change. Reference to heredity and "constitutional psychoses" made in the previous nomenclature, is eliminated, although it would seem that the latter term served a useful purpose.

001-x10 Manic-depressive psychoses

This group comprises the essentially benign, affective psychoses, mental disorders which fundamentally are marked by emotional oscillations and a tendency to recurrence. Various accessory symptoms such as illusions and "expectation" hallucinations may be added in individual cases to the fundamental affective alterations. To be distinguished are:

001-x11 Manic type with elevation of spirits (elation) or irritability, with overtalkativeness or flight of ideas and increased motor activity with the mental content expressed usually determined by objects or people in the environment. Transitory, often momentary, swings to depression may occur but should not change the classification from the predominantly manic type of reaction.

001-x12 Depressive type with outstanding depression of spirits and mental and motor retardation and inhibition; in some cases the mood is one of uneasiness and anxiety.

001-x13 Circular type. Here should be classified cases which show a change without a free or recovered interval of one phase to the opposite, i. e., when a manic reaction passes over into depressive reaction or vice versa.

001-x14 Mixed type. This term is not meant to apply to those cases that show transitory changes from depressive to elated moods or the reverse but is for those cases that show a combination of the cardinal symptoms of manic and depressive states. Perhaps the most frequent of these is the agitated depression, i. e., a depression of mood but with increased motor activity and at times pressure of thought. Occasionally also are seen cases of a so-called manic stupor in which there is elation and flight of ideas but with retarded motor activity amounting at times to complete immobility. Still other cases show elevation of mood and increased motor activity but without evident pressure of thought or flight of ideas, a so-called "unproductive mania." Many originally classed in this group differentiate finally into dementia præcox types.

001-x15 Perplexed type. In this type of reaction perplexity is an outstanding symptom in a depressive setting. Patients are apparently unable to understand their surroundings or they misinterpret them. Apparently as a result of this, they may show strange symptoms and bizarre behavior. The prognosis in general is good but the attacks may run a long course. Such patients are sometimes mistaken for cases of dementia præcox. The perplexity and general depressive reaction are differentiating features.

001-x16 Stuporous type. This reaction is characterized by a marked reduction in activity, at times leading to immobility. The mood is essentially one of depression and mutism may be present, and this with drooling and muscular symptoms at times suggests the catatonic form of dementia præcox. Retrospectively, however, it is found that the sensorium has been clouded and that there may have been ideas of death and dream-like hallucinations. Most psychiatrısts now consider these cases to be schizophrenic in nature, particularly when hallucinations are present.

001-x10 Other types. The above classification covers the majority of the manic-depressive reactions but occasionally there may be found some other type to be classified under this sub-group.

001-x20 Dementia præcox (schizophrenia)

Under this heading is classified the group of psychopathological reactions which may be acute and episodic, but more frequently are chronic and progressive, arising in persons who commonly have shown greater or lesser degrees of personality inadequacies. Such inadequacies are in the large proportion of cases demonstrated by tendencies to withdrawal from the realities of everyday life, inclinations to live in day-dreaming or phantasy, with shallowness of thought and judgment. Histories show that persons who develop dementia præcox reactions frequently retain immature ideas and feelings toward sexual life or have shown an inability to meet the demands of adult sexual adjustment. The symptoms of the more obvious disorder may be shown in a progressive withdrawal from contact with persons and activities in the environment. Or, on the personality groundwork, new adaptive demands or circumstances, which to the normal person would be ordinary, may precipitate symptoms which attract and demand attention, these manifesting themselves at times in excitement, again in stupor or phantastic delusional ideas, with hallucinations and with odd behavior which resembles often that of a child or primitive person. The reactions are spoken of, therefore, as regressions, a slipping-back to an earlier child-like or infantile type of feeling and acting.

This general group is divided into the following several subgroups because of the prominence of the various symptoms in individual cases, but it is to be borne in mind that these are only relative distinctions and transitions from one clinical form to another are common.

001-x21 Simple type. Cases to be classified under this heading show essentially defects of interest with gradual development of an apathetic state but without other strikingly peculiar behavior and without expression of delusions or hallucinations. They are prone to deterioration.

001-x22 Hebephrenic type. Cases to be classified under this heading show prominently a tendency to silliness, smiling, laughter which appears inconsistent with the ideas expressed; peculiar, often bizarre, ideas are expressed, neologisms or a coining of words or phrases not infrequently occur and hallucinations which appear pleasing to these individuals may be prominent.

001-x23 Catatonic type. These cases show prominence of negativistic reactions or various peculiarities of conduct with phases of stupor or excitement, the latter characterized often by impulsive or stereotyped behavior and usually hallucinations. It is found retrospectively that in the stupor the sensorium has remained clear. The excited types with pressure of speech and psychomotor acceleration are commonly mistaken for the manic phase of an affective disorder. The mental content as expressed is endogenous in origin, the environment playing only a minor rôle which differentiates the reaction from the manic type of production.

001-x24 Paranoid type. These cases are characterized by prominence of delusions, particularly ideas of persecution or grandeur and frequently with a consistent emotional reaction of aggressiveness due to persecution. There may be hallucinations in various fields to which the patients react at first consistently but later, as deterioration occurs, apathy or indifference may make an appearance. A predominantly homosexual component or fixation at this level of development appears prominent in this group of cases whereas the previous groups show evidence frequently of not having reached this level or of having regressed to more infantile levels of psychosexuality.

001-x20 Other types. Occasionally other types of reactions of dementia præcox may be found to be classified under this present heading.

001-x30 Paranoia

From this group should be excluded the deteriorating paranoic states (dementia præcox) and paranoid states symptomatic of other mental disorders, included under the organic brain disease, toxic and other groups. In the present group are to be classified those cases showing fixed suspicions and ideas of persecution logically elaborated for the most part after a false interpretation of an actual occurrence has been made. The emotional reactions are consistent with the ideas held and such persons are prone to take action against their persecutors, rendering them dangerous. Intelligence which is often of a superior type is well preserved. In this group belong certain types of reformers, agitators, litigious persons and prophets.

001-x31 Paranoid conditions

Cases in this group lie between the paranoia and paranoid dementia præcox groups in respect to the preservation of their personalities, coherence of their thinking and abnormalities in behavior. In this group should be classified those cases showing predominantly delusions, usually of a persecutory nature, with an inclination more toward illogical thinking and misinterpretation. Hallucinations may be prominent. Such conditions may exist for many years with little, if any, deterioration in general interests and with better preservation of the emotional reactions than in the paranoid form of dementia præcox.

001-x40 Psychoses with psychopathic personality

In this group are to be classified those cases that show abnormal reactions essentially of an emotional and volitional nature apparently on the basis of constitutional defect which are not to be classified under the groups already described. Cases of intellectual defect (feeblemindedness) are not to be included in this group.

Psychopathic personalities are characterized largely by emotional immaturity or childishness with marked defects of judgment and without evidence of learning by experience. They are prone to impulsive reactions without consideration of others and to emotional instability with rapid swings from elation to depression, often apparently for trivial causes. Special features in individual psychopaths are prominent criminal traits, moral deficiency, vagabondage and sexual perversions. Intelligence as shown by standard intelligence tests may be normal or superior, but on the other hand, not infrequently, a borderline intelligence may be present.

The abnormal reactions which bring psychopathic personalities into the group of psychoses are varied in form but usually of an episodic character. Most prominent are attacks of irritability, excitement, depression, paranoid episodes, transient confused states, etc. True prison psychoses belong in this group.

A psychopathic personality with a manic-depressive attack should be classed in the manic-depressive group and likewise a psychopathic personality with a schizophrenic psychosis should go in the dementia præcox group. Psychopathic personalities without episodic mental attack or psychotic symptoms should be placed in the group "Without psychosis."

001-x50 Psychoses with mental deficiency

Under this heading should be classified those mental defectives that show psychoses. These are usually of an acute transitory nature and most commonly are episodes of excitement or depression, paranoid trends or confused hallucinatory attacks. The degree of mental deficiency should be determined from the history and the use of the standard psychometric tests.

Mentally deficient persons may suffer from manic-depressive attacks or from dementia præcox or from the organic psychoses and they should be classified then under such respective headings instead of under the heading of mental deficiency. Cases of mental deficiency without psychotic disturbances should be placed in the group "Without psychosis."

Psychoneuroses

Hysteria

002-x00 Anxiety hysteria

There is not complete agreement on what should be covered by this designation. According to one viewpoint anxiety hysteria is conversion hysteria with anxiety added to the clinical picture. From another viewpoint anxiety hysteria includes those reactions which are indicated in the present classification under "Psychasthenia, phobia" (002-x23). From still another viewpoint, anxiety hysteria is not a desirable designation and all reactions which have been previously designated as anxiety hysteria are, according to this viewpoint, more properly classified as anxiety states (002-x33).

For statistical purposes patients showing conversion phenomena with recurring attacks of anxiety may be classified under anxiety hysteria. Other patients who present conversion symptoms or phobias but who are relatively free from recurring attacks of anxiety may be grouped under "Conversion hysteria" (002-x10) or "Psychasthenia, phobia" (002-x23).

002-x10 Conversion hysteria

Cases should be classified according to the sub-groups under this general heading. The symptoms to be found in these various types are indicated in the classification for guidance in differentiation and are self-explanatory. It is to be recalled, however, that some of these hysterical symptoms may occur in the psychoses, and by themselves are not diagnostic; the whole clinical history and picture must be considered.

Psychasthenia or compulsive states

Under this heading are to be classified those cases showing predominantly obsessions, compulsive acts, tics and spasms, and phobias; examples of frequent symptoms are given in the classification for guidance in differentiation.

002-x30 Neurasthenia

To be designated under this heading are those cases in which organic disease is ruled out and which develop motor and mental fatigability, diminished power of concentration and pressure in the head, scalp, neck or spine. Early dementia præcox or mild depressions of the manic-depressive type not infrequently have to be considered in the differential diagnosis.

002-x31 Hypochondriasis

Under this heading are to be classified those cases that show essentially an obsessive preoccupation with the state of their health or of various organs, with a variety of somatic complaints which are not relieved by demonstration of a lack of pathology. Occurring frequently in the involutional period, they are to be differentiated from involution melancholia by the absence of marked depression with agitation and self-condemnation. Hypochondriacal complaints may be a symptom of dementia præcox and this reaction type should be eliminated before classifying cases here.

002-x32 Reactive depression

Here are to be classified those cases which show depression in reaction to obvious external causes which might naturally produce sadness, such as bereavement, sickness and financial and other worries. The reaction, of a more marked degree and of longer duration than normal sadness, may be looked upon as pathological. The deep depression, with motor and mental retardation shown in the manic-depressive depressions, is not present, but these reactions may be more closely related in fact to the manic-depressive reactions than to the psychoneuroses.

002-x33 Anxiety state

Cases which show more or less continuous diffuse anxiety and apprehensive expectation, with paroxysmal exacerbations associated with physiological signs of fear, palpitation, dyspnea, nausea, diarrhoea, are to be classified here. Emotional tension is apt to be high, and irritability and intense self-preoccupation may be prominent, particularly during episodes. The diagnosis should not be made until all other more clearly defined types showing anxiety as a symptom have been excluded.

001-y00 *Undiagnosed psychoses*

In this group should be placed the cases in which a satisfactory diagnosis cannot be reasonably made and in which the psychosis must therefore be regarded as an unclassified one. Most frequently this may be due to lack of history, inaccessibility of the patient, or a too short period of observation. On the other hand, the clinical picture may be so obscured and the symptoms so unusual that a reasonably accurate classification cannot be made.

The number of undiagnosed psychoses may reflect the attitude of physicians, indicating either inadequacy of careful collection of facts and insufficient observation or, on the other hand, may indicate a too rigid tendency for absolute accuracy. It may be mentioned that reasonable accuracy and not absolute accuracy is looked for in statistical classification of medical conditions; this does not mean guessing at a classification or forcing one without reasonable facts.

0y0-y00 *Without mental disorder*

Attention is called to the note in the classification that this heading is to be used only in psychiatric hospitals. In these as well as in non-institutional practice the nonpsychotic condition which the patient shows is to be reported according to the designations in the classification. Disorders not named in the classification are to be specified under the heading "Other nonpsychotic diseases or conditions."

000-163 Disorders of personality due to epidemic encephalitis

Here are to be classified those cases that show comparatively mild changes in their personality as a result of epidemic encephalitis. These changes are not severe enough to handicap the individual in his relations with others. Erratic disordered behavior is not shown, intellect is not impaired and there is no marked emotional instability.

Cases showing character changes which disturb their relations with others and that show disordered erratic behavior, intellectual defects or marked emotional instability should be classified as "Psychosis with epidemic encephalitis" (003-163).

000-x40 Psychopathic personality

The symptoms listed in the classification are included as guides in the differentiation of the various types of psychopathic personality. Cases showing combinations of these traits should be classified under "Mixed types."

Psychopathic personalities showing episodes of excitement, depression, definite paranoid trends, hallucinatory states and other marked deviations from their usual personality reaction, should be classified as "Psychosis with psychopathic personality."

Primary behavior disorders

000-x61 Simple adult maladjustment

Under this heading are to be classified those cases which, without evidence of psychosis, or without a history of symptoms of psychopathic personality, appear nevertheless to be maladjusted, particularly to specific situations such as marriage, the home and occupation. Adaptability seems limited and such persons may be dependent more or less chronically on others for their support.

Primary behavior disorders in children

Under this heading attempt is made in the sub-groups to classify various disturbances seen in children which are primary and not secondary to disease or defect of the nervous system or other organic pathological states. One of the purposes of this classification is to separate them from the group "Without psychosis" under which they had been previously classified, particularly in institutions and clinics.

Cases showing definite clinical pictures of psychoneuroses, dementia præcox or manic-depressive reactions or other reaction types elsewhere classified, are to be placed under the appropriate headings in this classification and not under the present heading. It is expected therefore, that the group of so-called "problem children" who do not show definite symptomatology of recognized groups of mental disorders will be classified here.

It is obvious that there may be some overlapping in any one case of the symptoms of the various sub-groups but the cases should be classified according to the predominant behavior symptoms.

X I

CLASSIFICATION OF BEHAVIOR DISORDERS IN CHILDREN

A. MENTAL DEFICIENCIES (Indicate degree of feeblemindedness by terms *idiot, imbecile,* or *moron* in each case)

- I. Those due to brain defect or focal or diffuse destruction of brain tissue
  - a. Infections
    - 1. Syphilis
      - (a) Juvenile paretic neurosyphilis
      - (b) Cerebrospinal forms
    - 2. Forms of meningitis (specify type)
    - 3. Epidemic encephalitis
    - 4. Other forms (specify)
  - b. Traumatisms
    - 1. Birth injuries
    - 2. Other brain traumata
  - c. Congenital or developmental anomalies of central nervous system (specify type)
  - d. Special forms
    - 1. Hydrocephalus (congenital or acquired)
    - 2. Microcephalus
    - 3. Amaurotic family idiocy
    - 4. Congenital cerebral spastic infantile paralysis
    - 5. Choreo-athetoid conditions
  - e. Other forms (specify)
- II. Somatic types in which brain pathology is not the primary etiological factor (endocrine, metabolic, and other growth disturbances)
  - a. Cretinism
  - b. Childhood myxoedema
  - c. Dysgenital imbecility
  - d. Adiposity of hypophyseal origin with mental deficiency

III. Mongolism
IV. Tuberous sclerosis
V. Hereditary or cryptogenic types
VI. Undifferentiated

B. Psychoses

I. Psychoses due to somatic disorders
- a. Infectious diseases (delirious reactions)
  1. Acute infections
  2. Postencephalitic behavior disorders
  3. Syphilis
     - (a) Juvenile paretic neurosyphilis
     - (b) Cerebrospinal forms
- b. Traumata
  1. Cerebral trauma
  2. Posttraumatic reactions
- c. With other organic, focal, or diffuse brain destruction
- d. Intoxications
- e. Nutritional disturbances

II. Manic-depressive-like states
III. Schizophrenic-like states
IV. Reactive depressions
V. Undifferentiated
VI. Other varieties (specify)

C. Psychoneuroses and Neurotic Traits

I. Anxiety neuroses and states
- a. Acute diurnal attacks
- b. Nocturnal attacks
  1. Insomnia
  2. Somnambulism
  3. Night terrors

II. Neurasthenia
III. Conversion hysteria
IV. Anxiety hysteria

V. Obsessional-compulsion states
VI. Special phobias
VII. Transient reactions due to discomfort during or following somatic ailments

D. Convulsive Disorders
I. Symptomatic of known somatic disorders
II. Cryptogenic epilepsy
III. Jacksonian forms
IV. Other forms (specify)

E. Psychopathic Personality

F. Somatic Expressions of Personality Disorder Without a Known or Constant Anatomopathologic Basis
I. Hysterical paralyses, contractures, tremors, involuntary movements, tics, hyperkinesias, incoordination, limitations of motor functions, hysterical anesthesias, and other sensory disturbances
II. Migraine and other headaches
III. Pallor and fainting
IV. Asthma and other respiratory difficulties
V. Gastrointestinal disorders
a. Anorexia or compulsions to eat; food idiosyncrasies
b. Dysphagia
c. Gastric type of digestive disturbance; nausea; vomiting
d. Constipation; diarrhoea; soiling; mucous colitis
VI. Urinary dysfunction
a. Diurnal enuresis
b. Nocturnal enuresis
VII. Skin lesions
VIII. Other types (specify)

G. Special Behavior Disorders and Traits

I. Habit disorders
  a. Excessive masturbation
  b. Thumb sucking
  c. Nail biting
  d. Nose picking
  e. Clothes picking
  f. Fidgeting
  g. Others (specify)

II. Conduct disorders
  a. Obstinacy
  b. Rebellion
  c. Temper tantrums
  d. Destructiveness
  e. Cruelty
  f. Chronic aggressive reactions
  g. Chronic disobedience
  h. Delinquency
    1. Lying
    2. Stealing
    3. Wandering; vagrancy
    4. Truancy
    5. Setting fires
    6. Forgery
    7. Others (specify)

III. Sex perversions
  a. Homosexuality
  b. Sadism
  c. Exhibitionism
  d. Voyeurism
  e. Others (specify)

IV. Disabilities in reading

V. Disabilities in writing

VI. Disabilities in speech
   a. Due to organic motor disturbance
   b. Due to organic associative sensory-motor disturbance
   c. Due to organic auditory disturbance
   d. Traumatic speech neuroses
   e. Stammering; stuttering; lisping
   f. Delay in talking
   g. Speech characterized by neologisms and odd constructions

Definitions and Explanatory Notes

A. *Mental Deficiencies*

A diagnosis of mental deficiency is often possible by superficial observation, but in every case a careful study is necessary to determine possible causes, degree of defect and methods of management and treatment. Moreover, a detailed study is necessary for a diagnosis of doubtful cases. This survey should include a complete history and examination of the child. The psychometric examination is of much value in arriving at a diagnosis, but it should not be used as the sole criterion and should be interpreted in accordance with other findings.

When mental deficiency is complicated by a behavior disorder or other psychiatric problem the latter should be indicated in the diagnosis; for example, mental deficiency—familial type—moron with conduct disorder—truancy.

Although sharp lines of demarcation cannot be drawn between the several grades of mental deficiency the terms should be applied so far as possible in accordance with the following definitions, which have been adopted by the American Association on Mental Deficiency.

An *idiot* is a mentally-defective person usually having a mental age of less than 3 years or, if a child, an intelligence quotient of less than 20.

An *imbecile* is a mentally-defective person usually having a mental age of 3 years to 7 years inclusive, or, if a child, an intelligence quotient from 20 to 49 inclusive.

A *moron* is a mentally-defective person usually having a mental age of 8 years or upwards, or, if a child, an intelligence quotient of 50 or more. As a rule the upper limit for a diagnosis of mental deficiency should be an intelligence quotient of 69, but this limit should not be adhered to in cases where medical, social and other factors clearly indicate that the patient is mentally defective.

For purposes of this classification, in computing intelligence quotients of adults, the mental age is to be divided by 16.

The intelligence quotients mentioned above are based on the use of the Stanford Revision of the Binet-Simon Test.

Borderline cases, including cases with intelligence quotients between 70 and 79, should not be regarded as mentally defective unless the diagnosis can be definitely established on other grounds.

I. Those due to brain defect or focal or diffuse destruction of brain tissue.

a. *Infections.* Under this heading are included those cases of mental deficiency in which an infectious process was the causative agent. It is necessary in each instance, if possible, to specify the infection or infectious disease which acted as the etiological factor when a case of mental deficiency is classified under this type.

Among the subtopics of this heading, cases of mental deficiency due to congenital syphilis are to be classified. It is important to remember that congenital syphilis may co-exist with mental deficiency in the same patient and yet not have any causative relationship. When the mental level of the patient is appreciably below that of the general mental level of the family stock and there is congenital syphilis in the patient, without direct central nervous system infection, the indications are that the syphilis bears a causative relation to the mental defect through its blastophoric effects. In other cases of mental deficiency with congenital syphilis, there are found evidences of a direct infection of the central nervous system as shown by positive spinal fluid findings or neurological signs, or both; some cases of hydrocephalus are the result of a syphilitic basilar meningitis.

Meningitis is of importance as a causative agent in mental deficiency only when it is accompanied by an encephalitic process or when it results in adhesions which obstruct the circulation of the cerebrospinal fluid. In the latter instance, a secondary hydrocephalus is apt to occur. Epidemic encephalitis may be a cause of intelligence arrest, and other types of encephalitis are not an uncommon complication of infectious diseases of childhood, especially measles, scarlet fever, and whooping cough.

b. *Traumatisms.* The cases classifiable under this heading are those in which some brain damage occurred during birth. The brain of the child is particularly liable to injury at birth in cases of difficult and prolonged labor resulting in various degrees of gross physical and mental damage. The injury may be a tearing of the blood vessels, such as the longitudinal or lateral sinuses, or the result of a prolonged anoxemia on the delicate cortical cells.

On occasion, skull fractures and severe concussions incurred in infancy and early childhood may result in an arrest of intelligence development. In addition to neurological symptoms these patients usually have an irritable and excitable make-up.

c. *Congenital or Developmental Anomalies of the Central Nervous System.* Feeblemindedness due to various embryological arrests or distortions in parts of the brain as indicated by the neurological findings and the somatic development are classified in this group. Some of the special forms are mentioned below.

d. *Special Forms.* There are several different types of cranial anomalism such as microcephalus, hydrocephalus, oxycephalus, and others. When any of these appear to be expressions of a developmental inferiority, the case is to be classified under this heading and in every instance the particular cranial anomaly is to be specified.

Amaurotic family idiocy, with its syndrome of mental enfeeblement usually accompanied by spastic paralysis of all extremities and progressive blindness and with an onset anywhere from the age of a few months to 10 years, and allied states; congenital cerebral spastic infantile paralysis, characterized by a bilateral rigidity involving all voluntary musculature, with usually a small skull and general underdevelopment (care must be taken not to confuse such cases with the traumatic types occurring at birth); the various choreo-athetoid conditions, forms of Schilder's disease, and Friedreich's ataxia are among the typical examples of these special forms.

II. Somatic types in which brain pathology is not the primary etiological factor.

This heading indicates endocrine metabolic disturbances as such and some other growth disorders in which brain disease *per se* is not the cause although the brain and other parts of the nervous system may become involved and reveal severe lesions in some types. Patients with cretinism, hypothyroidism, pituitary dystrophy, and well-defined polyglandular disturbances should be classified here. It is important, however, to remember that not a few of the familial (hereditary) types show endocrinopathies; in such instances the case is to be classified under the familial type.

Among the examples of this group of disorders are *endemic and sporadic cretinism,* a complex of somatic and mental disturbance with changes in the skin, skeleton, and nervous system, with retardation of the development of the mind; *childhood myxoedema,* a chronic condition due to a markedly diminished function of the thyroid gland beginning before birth or very early in life and causing physical and mental deficiencies; and *genital deficiencies, Froelich's syndrome,* and the *Lawrence-Moon-Biedl syndrome.*

III. Mongolism, so-called because of the resemblance of the patient to the mongolian race.

The cause of this anomaly is still unknown but it is recognized by a combination of several characteristic physical traits in association with imbecility or idiocy. In infants care must be used in distinguishing between mongolism and cretinism. So-called "mongoloid states," if not sufficiently distinct to be regarded as mongolism, should not be included here.

IV. Tuberous Sclerosis.

This is a relatively rare developmental condition of the brain and other organs characterized clinically by a retrograde mental defect, sometimes with epilepsy, and pathologically by multiple sclerotic nodes over the surface of the brain, subependymal tumors and multiple lesions of the skin, heart, kidneys, and other organs. The disease is congenital but neither familial nor hereditary. Such children may have been normal, active, and intelligent during their early years, although the disease is thought to begin in the early foetal months.

V. Hereditary or Cryptogenic Types.

To be included here are those cases in which mental deficiency in the family appears to have a direct relation to the defective state of the patient. Such cases may be of the imbecile or the moron types, but rarely of the idiot level. Endocrine dysfunction may be found in such cases. Some seem to occur sporadically without a detectable family taint.

VI. Undifferentiated.

There are, of course, a large number of mentally deficient individuals who cannot be placed under any of the foregoing clinical types. They are not differentiated either by symptomatology, pathogenesis, or cause.

B. *Psychoses*

With the exception of those due to acute somatic disorders, psychoses are relatively infrequent in children. Mental reactions to acute infections and intoxications are usually transient in character with delirium, hallucinatory episodes, clouding of consciousness, disorientation, haziness, and fear. Patients with encephalitis from whatever cause may be considered psychotic whenever the conduct is so changed as to appear irrational. Spinal fluid examinations are often necessary in order to diagnose syphilogenic disorders. A diagnosis of schizophrenic-like and manic-depressive-like disorders should be made only after other possibilities are ruled out. Conduct disorders, compulsive acts, overlively imaginations, and particularly severe hysterical syndromes should not be confused with schizophrenia or other psychoses. Manic-like attacks are often seen in those children with organic brain disease. Owing to the fact that many psychiatrists still doubt that the affective and schizophrenic psychoses of children are identical with those found in adults, it may be well to use, for example, the term "schizophrenic-like" until further research has illuminated this field.

C. *Psychoneuroses and Neurotic Traits*

All types of psychoneuroses, including anxieties, hysteria, obsessions, compulsions, phobias, and other psychoneurotic states, are found in children. Obsessions and compulsions are not infrequently overlooked as children are reticent about discussing their symptoms. These are sometimes seen early in childhood and are common during the latency period. In addition to the usual psychoneurotic reactions, conduct such as compulsive stealing which may be evidence of a neurosis, is not infrequently seen. This type of compulsive conduct should be clearly distinguished from the more usual forms of conduct disorder. Many undesirable traits in children, such as nail biting, do not in themselves constitute neuroses and should be classified under habit disorders.

D. *Convulsive Disorders*

Convulsive states in children are frequently on a symptomatic basis. They may be the result of toxic states, of acute infectious diseases or other illnesses, or the residual of an organic injury to the brain at birth. Petit mal, grand mal, and other types of convulsions occur in childhood, but a diagnosis of epilepsy in any form should not be made without an adequate history and a careful examination. A diagnosis of idiopathic or cryptogenic epilepsy should only be made after all possible physical causes are ruled out. The epilepsies may produce or be associated with early mental deterioration.

E. *Psychopathic Personality*

Mental conditions suggesting the presence of an inherent psychopathic personality are occasionally seen in children. Care should be taken in making this diagnosis in children, however, unless the facts clearly indicate it. So-called psychopathic symptoms seen in children are frequently transient, and may depend upon environmental rather than inherent conditions. Even when psychopathic symptoms have been continuously present from a very early age, it is as a rule unsafe to make a diagnosis of a psychopathic personality in any child under ten years of age. These states should not be confused with true psychopathic states as seen in adults.

A distinction between psychoneuroses, psychopathic personality, and neurotic traits can be made by careful consideration of all of the facts of the case.

F. *Somatic Expressions of Personality Disorder Without a Known or Constant Anatomopathologic Basis*

Disorders should not be placed in this group unless the positive signs of a psychological disturbance are found to be present. Since conversion manifestations may resemble any organic illness, great care should be taken in making a differential diagnosis. Proceedings for distinguishing hysterical motor and sensory symptoms from those due to organic lesions may be found in any comprehensive textbook on neurology. Often an extensive experience in organic disease in childhood is necessary to enable the physician to make a correct diagnosis of some of the somatic expressions encountered. When a physical examination has excluded or made doubtful a possible organic origin or present basis of the trouble, a thorough search for the signs of psychogenic disorder should be made by examining any anxieties connected with the onset of symptoms, the emotional relationships with those at home, and pertinent facts regarding the character and personality of the child. The subheadings indicate a number of symptom expressions of psychic conflicts.

G. *Special Behavior Disorders and Traits*

This general group of special phenomena is outlined to embrace different forms of disorder in the field of behavior, namely: habit disorders, conduct disorders, sex perversions, and some particular disabilities. It is believed that these subdivisions permit a more satisfactory designation of conditions found than would otherwise be possible. Cases may be classified under this heading only when no other well-defined psychiatric disorder is present.

I. Habit Disorders.

These are particularly prevalent during the preschool period, although they occur at all ages. They are often minor and transient in character in young children. In older children they may be more permanent. They may be the result of the lack of proper training or they may be the expression of complexes and mental conflicts. A distinction between habit disorders, psychoneuroses, and neurotic traits is generally possible. Habit disorders are often represented by the repetition of simple acts in which the emotional component is very slight, whereas neurotic traits have a strong emotional coloring and less often follow a distinct habit pattern.

II. Conduct Disorders.

These cover a wide range of misconduct from minor misbehavior to grave delinquency. Such conditions may exist in the home, in the school, or in the community. They may arise chiefly within the child or they may be dependent upon environmental influences. They are to be regarded as secondary phenomena when seen in cases of mental deficiency, epilepsy, encephalitis, and other well recognized organic diseases. The term "conduct disorder" is not generally applied to very young children.

III. Sex Perversions.

The designations mentioned here are to be used in classifying those occasional cases of sexual maladjustment which have become established in the childhood period as an outstanding problem or feature in the social life of the child.

IV and V. Disabilities in Reading and Writing.

These special mental disabilities are found in respect to reading and occasionally writing and number work. Their existence, unrecognized by teachers, may account for slow progress in school. These special disabilities, however, should not be confused with general backwardness or retardation which exists in dull or defective children. Such a disability may be diagnosed by means of standardized tests which have been specially devised for their recognition. A relationship between these conditions and similar disorders found in aphasia has been described.

VI. Disabilities in Speech.

This category has been added and arranged to include those cases where a disorder of speech is the only or the most striking expression of some underlying difficulty. The subtopics are intended to cover most of the types usually encountered in practice.

avior to grave delinquency. Such conditions
in the home, in the school, or in the community.
arise chiefly within the child or they may be depe
environmental influences. They are to be regarde
ondary phenomena when seen in cases of mental di
epilepsy, encephalitis, and other well recognized
diseases. The term "conduct disorder" is not com
plied to very young children.

III. Sex Perversions.

The designations mentioned here are to be used i
fying those occasional cases of sexual maladjus
have become established in the childhood period a
standing problem or feature in the social life of t

IV and V. Disabilities in Reading and Writi

These special mental disabilities are found in
reading and occasionally writing and number work
existence, unrecognized by teachers, may account f
progress in school. These special disabilities, h
should not be confused with general backwardnes
tardation which exists in dull or defective childre
a disability may be diagnosed by means of stan
tests which have been specially devised for their
tion. A relationship between these conditions and
disorders found in aphasia has been described.

VI. Disabilities in Speech.

This category has been added and arranged to
those cases where a disorder of speech is the only
most striking expression of some underlying difficul
subtopics are intended to cover most of the types u
countered in pediatrics.

CPSIA information can be obtained
at www.ICGtesting.com
Printed in the USA
BVHW041035210219
540828BV00009B/467/P

9 781397 308832